More Advance Praise for
The Optimistic Workplace

"Stewardship—not a word we often use in business but one we should and must. The best leaders, the best managers, are actually stewards. With the dramatic reshaping of our global economy, the lack of a return to normalcy, a generation in the workforce that verbalizes their desire for meaning *and* money, not just money, it's time to use the language of stewardship. Shawn's book helps us understand why now is the time and how we can make stewardship real. Read it, do it!"

—Deb Mills-Scofield

"Shawn Murphy has an inspiring and insightful way of sharing how optimism changes everything in the workplace. His stories and examples take optimism out of a concept and into a guide for changing how we work, lead, and collaborate. I recommend this book for any leader intent on building an optimistic culture and for anyone ready to connect purpose to their work. *The Optimistic Workplace* is a wonderful read that reminds us not only why we need more optimism and meaning in our work—but how to find it!"

—Patti Johnson, CEO of PeopleResults and author of *Make Waves: Be the One to Start Change at Work and in Life*

"Shawn Murphy has written an unabashedly optimistic and utterly practical guide to making our work (and life) more fulfilled—a must-read for everybody who is seeking to create a more human enterprise."

—Tim Leberecht, author of *The Business Romantic*

"Shawn reminds readers that creating environments where employees can flourish, feel fulfilled, and actually grow into better versions of themselves is more than a 'nice to have.' This is the new paradigm, and it is incumbent upon all business leaders to adopt it. *The Optimistic Workplace* not only provides examples of organizations whose leaders are answering that call, but informs and inspires others to join the movement."

—David Hassell, Founder & CEO, 15Five

THE
OPTIMISTIC
WORKPLACE

*Creating an Environment That
Energizes Everyone*

Shawn Murphy

Foreword by Dorie Clark

⁄AMACOM

American Management Association
New York • Atlanta • Brussels • Chicago • Mexico City • San Francisco
Shanghai • Tokyo • Toronto • Washington, D.C.

Bulk discounts available. For details visit:
www.amacombooks.org/go/specialsales
Or contact special sales:
Phone: 800-250-5308
Email: specialsls@amanet.org
View all the AMACOM titles at: www.amacombooks.org
American Management Association: www.amanet.org

This publication is designed to provide accurate and authoritative information in regard to the subject matter covered. It is sold with the understanding that the publisher is not engaged in rendering legal, accounting, or other professional service. If legal advice or other expert assistance is required, the services of a competent professional person should be sought.

LIBRARY OF CONGRESS CATALOGING-IN-PUBLICATION DATA

Murphy, Shawn
  The optimistic workplace : creating an environment that energizes everyone / Shawn Murphy.
    pages cm
  Includes index.
  ISBN 978-0-8144-3619-6 (hardcover) -- ISBN 978-0-8144-3620-2 (ebook) 1. Work environment. I. Title.
  HD7261.M87 2015
  658.3'12--dc23
                        2015025460

About AMA
American Management Association (www.amanet.org) is a world leader in talent development, advancing the skills of individuals to drive business success. Our mission is to support the goals of individuals and organizations through a complete range of products and services, including classroom and virtual seminars, webcasts, webinars, podcasts, conferences, corporate and government solutions, business books, and research. AMA's approach to improving performance combines experiential learning—learning through doing—with opportunities for ongoing professional growth at every step of one's career journey.

Printing number

10 9 8 7 6 5 4 3 2 1

This book is dedicated to Randy.
Sweets, you are my balance in this chaotic world.

Contents

Foreword

THE BEST PLACES TO WORK HAVE IT. THE HIGHEST-PERFORMING teams benefit from it. Because of it, individuals thrive professionally and personally—and teams and organizations flourish in our new economy.

The "it" I'm referring to?

The climate of your workplace. The feeling. The mood. "It" is the chemistry of how you, your team, and your organization work together.

The way your workplace "feels" has a tremendous influence on people's experience, morale, and performance. People thrive in a climate where they feel valued, where they know their contributions are meaningful, and where their core values are closely aligned with the values and character of their employer. Where they don't feel valued, meaningful, and aligned . . . they just do their jobs. And today, in a world where opportunities to stand out are everywhere and the next killer idea can come from anywhere, "just doing our jobs" isn't good enough.

They need more. And we, as leaders, need more.

It is the leaders, however, that must take the first step.

First, we need to start thinking of our people as human beings eager to make a difference in the world, not as mere "human capital." Next, we must set out to make sure every individual, team, department, product, and service center knows they are directly contributing to the mission. Along the way, we must serve as shepherds of our culture. And finally: We must create an environment that energizes every member of our team.

In short: We must deliberately create an optimistic workplace.

Yes, some of us have lost the fire in our bellies for such bold thinking. Some of us are ready to just ride out the rest of our careers, satisfied with just doing our jobs.

I believe, though, that the fire isn't lost. It's just forgotten. Or perhaps buried in Industrial Age thinking where creativity was buried under piles of conformity.

Often, we don't even remember what it feels like to be inspired. To be part of the solution. To serve others. To simultaneously do good work *and* do the right thing. We've grown accustomed to ignoring the *human* side of business. So we tolerate the status quo. Each day, we metaphorically clock in—and then proceed to plod along doing unremarkable things for eight, ten, twelve hours per day. And, soon, without even realizing it, we accept that in a workplace that steals our mojo, there's no room for breakthrough ideas, invigorating relationships, or aha moments.

And so it goes for too many organizations.

Work environments have become modern-day factories that focus exclusively on production cycles, meeting quotas, and making sure the quarterly report pleases, or at least appeases, the shareholders and stakeholders. Where the work gets done, but only as required—and without any magic, without any soul.

The workplace requires reinvention.

We must become human again. We must give ourselves permission to not only enjoy our work, but bring our souls along with us.

Some companies are already taking this bold step. And in this thought-provoking book by Shawn Murphy, we get to see the impact the leaders of those organizations are having on their workplace environments. Shawn profiles people like Mark Bertolini of Aetna and Mark Fernandes of Luck Companies as well as organizations like Zingerman's, Google, and HopeLab. All of them are doing amazing work by motivating people—the right way—to achieve stellar business results.

Through his research on workplaces that have deliberately created optimistic cultures (and those that should), Shawn has developed principles that successful leaders can employ *right now* to create a genuinely optimistic workplace.

And his timing couldn't be better.

Our workplaces desperately need a healthy dose of optimism.

As Shawn has laid before us in the pages that follow, workplace optimism is a transformative influence. How your workplace feels ("climate") and acts ("culture") can, and does, motivate us to build great teams—and do great things. He shows us that collective optimism is not just a way to stand out, it's a core element of the human side of business. And when you bring people together around a common cause, it doesn't just impact your workplace: It can begin to change our communities—and our world.

As you read the pages of this book, I challenge you to think about your role.

How will you personally embrace the power an optimistic workplace wields? How will you make a real difference for your organization? More profoundly, how will you turn the heads and awaken the hearts of those you lead? How will you change their minds—and lives?

As you read *The Optimistic Workplace*, you'll discover: With optimism as a defining trait of our workplaces, good things happen. When optimism is rooted in purpose and deliberately and carefully surrounded by a positive work environment, nothing is impossible.

That is the message of Shawn's book. And after immersing yourself in these ideas, it's my hope that you'll feel inspired to share that message with your colleagues and all the people you influence and lead. Optimism is contagious, and it can change our workplaces and lives for the better.

DORIE CLARK
Author of *Stand Out* and *Reinventing You* and adjunct professor,
Fuqua School of Business, Duke University

Acknowledgments

IT WAS IN MR. LLOYD'S CLASS THAT I HAD MY FIRST STORY READ out loud. I was in fifth grade. I was awkward, skinny, and invisible, or so I thought. I was enthralled with J. R. R. Tolkien's *The Hobbit*. I had written a short story that riffed on Tolkien's books. Mr. Lloyd liked it and asked my permission to read it aloud to my classmates. I agreed. I don't recall if anyone paid attention. I was too embarrassed to notice. In hindsight, that childhood moment is when writing became interesting to me.

Today with a few more pounds on me and a bit more confidence in myself, I offer to you my next story. I'm humbled, not embarrassed. What you hold in your hand is a community effort. There are many people who have guided, coached, and encouraged me to create what you're about to read. Writing is hardly a solo act. This book is a result of many people's efforts, late nights, plane flights, and sacrifices. So indulge me as I express my gratitude to the community that helped me create this book.

This book's journey begins with my friend Alejandro Reyes. He reignited the writer's passion in me by encouraging me to start a blog. Coupled with Alejandro's encouragement was my friend Karen Martin's insistence that I write a book. It was as if Alejandro passed the baton to Karen to ensure I relived the secret thrill I kept to myself when my fifth-grade story was read aloud. Karen, you went to bat for me and helped me get John Willig as my agent. Thank you for believing in me. Alejandro, thank you for all the encouragement.

John, thank you for guiding me through the steps to get a publisher. You were very gracious in the way you shared the many denials from editors. And I am thankful for your guidance. Being a first-time author is overwhelming. You helped make it less so.

I do believe things happen for a reason. My editor, Stephen S. Power, believed and understood the purpose behind this book project from the beginning. Stephen, I appreciate your direction and insight through the multiple rounds of edits. The examples in the book are stronger and its structure is better than the zero draft I sent you.

I want to thank the team at AMACOM for helping me get this book ready for market. Erika Spelman, you helped make the copyedit phase tolerable. More important, however, is the way you surgically went in and found ways to make my writing clearer and crisper. Janet Pagano, thank you for your marketing guidance. Ron Silverman, your edits were spot on. Thanks also to Irene Majuk, AMACOM's director of publicity. Sabrina Bowers, you sacrificed time on the weekend to ensure we kept to our schedule. Thank you. And Holly Fairbank, you helped put the finishing touches on this manuscript. I'm grateful.

So here's a confession. I'm a horrible procrastinator. Because of it I lost out on multiple rounds of feedback from reviewers—friends who graciously offered to read crappy versions of the manuscript. Thank you to Deb Mills-Scofield, Liz Butler, Malek Hadad, and Mark Babbitt. Your initial feedback encouraged me to dig deeper in my writing. The first version of the few chapters I sent you were stinkers.

Writing a book is an all-consuming experience. I wasn't available to people at times when they would have preferred I be with them. So thank you to my wonderful team at Switch & Shift—Beth Nicoletto and Lauren Kirkpatrick—for keeping things moving forward the many times I needed to miss our one-on-ones and meetings. I already mentioned Mark Babbitt, my friend and business partner. But thank you, sir, for holding the fort down as I played Ernest Hemingway.

Being a newbie writer isn't glamorous. I had to work to pay the bills and find time to write. There were times when I skipped client work to write. Thank you Lee Scott, Nicole Welch, Tiffany Rolston, Linda Nedney, Tina Shaw, Nancy Wright, David Kendall, Bill Otterbeck, Julie Murata, and Peter Kelly for not calling me out when I missed meetings with you.

Here's another confession. I get bored easily and have a short attention span. Because of that I had to leave my house and check into a hotel to write with fewer distractions. Thank you to the amazing staff at The Citizen Hotel in Sacramento. You helped me be more disciplined in meeting my writing deadlines. I want to give a special shout-out to Mark and Tracy at The Grange. Your two happy faces were a treat after staring at my computer screen for hours.

I can't forget to thank my mom, dad, and stepmom and stepdad. You never made me feel bad for going months without checking in.

No other person felt the impact of my absence more than my love, Randy. Sweets, not once did you complain about my lack of availability. And even when we were spending time together, my mind was working over a difficult sentence or a troubled section of the book. You held the house together and made room for me to write. You always make room for this dreamer to, well, dream. Thank you. I love you.

I have to give a shout-out to our cat, Palmer. He is my writing buddy.

Finally, thank you, God. This journey started and will continue with you.

Introduction

STUDS TERKEL'S CLASSIC 1972 BOOK *WORKING* OPENS WITH A drab, sullen note that still seems too familiar today: "This book, being about work, is, by its very nature, about violence—to the spirit as well as to the body."[1] For centuries, workers have endured treatment that belittles their pride and robs the artistry from their craft. All the while "the man," sticking it to his employees, kept a greedy eye on profits while ignoring working conditions. People were merely a means to a profitable end.

This is not Terkel's tome continued. This is my shot across the bow against the archaic beliefs still squandering people's hopes, ideas, humanity, and access to meaningful work. I'm not the first to fire, but one of many emboldened by the belief that work can be a source of fulfillment, joy, and happiness. Business leaders like Menlo Innovation's Rich Sheridan, Luck Companies' Mark Fernandes and Charlie Luck, Zingerman's Ari Weinzweig, and Barry-Wehmiller's Bob Chapman are uniting balance sheets and people-centric business philosophies to astonishing results. They are infusing a different heart and soul into their companies and rewriting the rule book of what business success looks like and what it means. For these leaders, success is also defined by how employees experience the workday in their organization. These leaders and many others are featured in this book as examples of what human-centered businesses look like on the inside.

I don't like the term *manager*. In a conversation with CEO Bob Chapman at Barry-Wehmiller, he asked me to promise I wouldn't use the word in this book. I nearly fulfilled my promise. The role of manager is long associated with command and control, a better-than attitude that is hauntingly recounted by Terkel. We don't have time or room for this type of manager anymore. Work is personal, and it needs to be a contribution to people's lives. And it's not managers who make that happen.

Now I know this might be alarming, especially given that this book is written for those of you pushed and pulled in the middle layer of a hierarchy. I'm not advocating that the work of those once-labeled *managers* go away. I'm advocating that you fulfill a higher calling than looking over the shoulders of your employees to see that they get their work done.

The higher calling that I'm whispering not so quietly into your ear is to create an environment that positions people to do their best work and also become better human beings. I know that some of you will find this book supporting what you're already doing. In short, you're not commanding anyone. You're coming alongside people and learning how best to support them. I believe you'll find the elements of an optimistic workplace to be a good addition to your leadership repertoire and philosophy.

Whenever I told friends and strangers the idea behind the optimistic workplace, I heard the same response: "We need that where I work." Even without explaining the nuance in what I'm writing about, this response told me one thing: We long to feel good about our work. In his brilliant way of writing, Studs Terkel explained over 40 years ago what people wanted from their work efforts: "It is about a search, too, for daily meaning as well as daily bread, for recognition as well as cash, for astonishment rather than torpor; in short for a sort of life rather than a Monday through Friday sort of dying. . . . To be remembered was the wish, spoken and unspoken, of the heroes and heroines of this book."[2]

When we show up at work we want to be seen, as Pat Christen, CEO of the nonprofit HopeLab, told me. If you think about it, we all want our work-time investment to matter. You hold the key to this. Instead of work robbing your employees' souls of something good each day, you can play a positive part that helps them live up to their potential. Throughout this book are ideas to help optimism emerge in the workplace that are plucked from the companies featured in it, from my consulting work, and from what research is uncovering in terms of positive workplaces.

This book is about modeling the expectations necessary to contribute to the emergence of optimism in the work environment. It's not about being or becoming an optimist. Optimistic workplaces need diversity in perspective and in people from all backgrounds and inclinations.

What unites them is a workplace mood that gives hope that good things are possible from applying one's experiences to ultimately help the organization create value for its customers.

THE EVOLUTION OF MANAGEMENT

This is not a book for managers—at least as we've come to understand the term. *Management* and *managers* are loaded words that come with baggage and conclusions that no longer benefit a business or its people. Rather, this is a book for and about people who want to evolve management and business. This is a book for stewards. Mark Fernandes, chief leadership officer at Luck Companies, defines stewardship as caring for people and things that don't belong to you.

Conversely, the term *management* is associated with control and dominance: "I need to manage you." Or, "You're my subordinate, and because of my years of experience, I know what's best. Do as I say."

You are the steward of your people, of resources and time, and of the business. The subtle shift is in the focus. It isn't about the control you flex, the dominance you project, or the power you wield. It's about purposefully crafting a work environment that allows the human side of business to flourish. The shift is in caring for people in a way that improves their lives and positively influences the value they create for your organization. In a way, this book is about our human nature and the rich insights it holds to positively influence people and business.

Why do we need to evolve from management? Brilliant minds like Gary Hamel, Raj Sisodia, and Rosabeth Moss Kanter provide sage insights into evolving management to be more conscious, to be more human. The truth is, management has become soulless. It's rote. It's impersonal. Why is that important? Simply put, business has always been and will always be about relationships.

So far I've focused on relationships with customers and shareholders. But I've not spent enough time on the relationship with employees. Stewardship is rooted in the pursuit of mutually beneficial outcomes. Gary Hamel writes about stewardship in the opening of *What Matters Now*. In it he distinguishes stewards as having responsibility for a greater good and not succumbing to the allure of self-interest.[3]

Language is how we make sense of the world; it's how we find meaning to what we hear and see. To evolve management and still use its label keeps its rusty hooks in our thoughts, reminding us of what was. So we'll stumble our way through shifting language away from the term *manager*. We need to be intentional about the words we use. They create realities. From this point forward, I'll use a variety of words: *coach, mentor, leader, guide*. But primarily, the evolution of management is stewardship.

A steward takes her responsibilities to guide, coach, mentor, and lead her team with awareness of how her presence helps and hinders. A steward doesn't manage. She inspires. She motivates. She inquires. She notices. She supports. She partners. Supervisor Larry Robillard of Zingerman's explained that his role is to facilitate greatness in his people through his actions and words.[4] This isn't an arrogant statement. It's delivered with genuine care for people.

The idea of stewardship in business is not mine originally. Peter Block writes about it in his book *Stewardship*. In it he explains how irrelevant the management actions of controlling, goal setting with the assumption that people can't set their own, and shifting accountability to the leader for results are outdated and a disservice to employees. Block writes, "People who leave their minds at home and bring their bodies to work will destroy us."[5] This is the epitome of management that no longer serves in the best interest of the organization and its people. More than that, however, is it's an insult to employees' intelligence.

We have veered too far away from hiring and treating employees as mature, fully functioning adults. Stewards create workplace contexts that assume people can be trusted to do their best work and to do the right thing. We've gone too long in treating people as though they need to be controlled if we want them to do what we need.

Notice the word *we*. This, too, is what's reinforced with the construct of stewardship. Business success does not come from what management wants but from what the team can create and accomplish together. The divisive relationship between stewards and employees cripples a business's ability to be adaptable, be agile, and deliver value needed to sustain itself.

The human-centered business is fundamentally built on a foundation of helping people understand and leverage their potential for good—a good that benefits others. The good you can bring about is a positive work experience created through workplace optimism.

Reflect back on the powerful influence Franklin Roosevelt had on America with his tangible vision of a country back on its feet and people contributing financially to their families. He had to believe that a better future was possible. More than that, he *wanted* a better future.

What about you? What does a better future look like for your team? Your organization?

In Appendix 1 you will find the Optimism Planner. It's a guided plan that will walk you through the steps necessary for you to create an optimistic workplace. It has three sections:

1. The First 30 Days—Planning

2. The Next 30 Days—Implementation

3. The Final 30 Days—Monitoring

You can complete the planner in a variety of ways. You can read through the book from front to back and then go through the planner. Another option is to read each part of the book and then go to the planner, completing each section.

Some of you may power through the Optimism Planner, answering the questions in a few days. I encourage you to read through the book and then pace yourself in answering the questions. This approach will help you savor the material and reflect on what's most important to you and your circumstances.

In the end, however, I encourage you to go through the Optimism Planner in a manner most suitable to your goals.

CHAPTER 1

The Future of the Workplace

Of all human talents, among the most precious ones is this ability
to discern opportunities around oneself, when others do not.
—MIHALY CSIKSZENTMIHALYI, *FLOW*

FORGET ABOUT CULTURE.
HOW'S THE CLIMATE?

In an underground space with no windows, the sound levels from conversations among team members are at first alarming but become charming. It's an oddity, in the open workspace, to have something that can be described as "charming." The casual observer may not see it. Only when you listen to what's happening and soak in the industrial funkiness of the workspace does the charm become evident. The noise becomes white. The fervent conversations reveal intelligence, creativity, fun, connection, and even creative disagreements. The employees at Menlo Innovations in Ann Arbor, Michigan, love what they do, and where they do it fits their culture like a well-tailored suit, but you'll not find anyone dressed in a suit or even wearing a tie.

Menlo Innovations is a software-development company, its name inspired by Thomas Edison's factory once in Menlo Park, New Jersey. There are no managers overseeing the work. Instead, team members work collaboratively. When I ask some Menlonians (their term) who the boss is, there is no consistent answer. Even the founders are not unanimously thought to be chief anything. Though they have titles with *chief* in the name, they are treated as part of the team, not differently.

Serving as a meeting reminder, a dartboard hung on the wall signals all team members to stop what they're doing and form a large circle. One Menlonian grabs a two-horned Viking hat and brings it to the circle. In less than 15 minutes, 50 or so people share project and company updates. All the information is relevant. People pay attention. As for the Viking hat? Well, everyone works in pairs every day at Menlo. For the stand-up meeting, each working pair holds a horn and gives an update. The hat is then passed to the next pair. Think of the Viking hat as an updated version of the talking stick.

What's described above are elements of Menlo's culture a la the tradition of a stand-up meeting facilitated by a Viking hat. Culture is how things are done in an organization.[1] It's the company's history, stories passed down over time. It's cultural artifacts like the Viking hat. As another example of culture, consider Menlo's hiring approach. Large groups of potential candidates are brought in and paired with one simple instruction: Make the other person look good. Menlo's interview process is how it weeds out those who wouldn't fit into its highly team-oriented culture.

Yet what is equally important as culture is what it feels like to work day to day in the workplace. This is climate, and it's the element of organizational life that isn't discussed much. Harvard University psychologists Robert Stringer and George Litwin explain climate as the quality of the workplace environment and its influence on the work experience and team members' behaviors and perceptions.[2]

Think of organizational climate like walking into a party that you're excited to attend. You arrive and feel the buzz from the lively crowd and happy music. You see people you want to meet. The feeling of excitement is palpable. You smile and allow yourself to enjoy the festivities. Of course the opposite could be true. You may have to attend as an obligation and arrive to the party feeling overwhelmed by the crowd and loud music. A feeling of dismay might overcome you as you find a quiet place in the party away from the crowd. Ultimately, the degree to which you enjoy the party depends on your expectations. Even previous experiences shape your perception of the party. But your perception of the party can be changed. How? The people at the party can make a fun party a blast or help you loosen up to enjoy the festivities.

Now take the party example and place it in an organizational context. How do people view your leadership style? How do you use your style to influence the climate? What does it feel like to work in your team? These questions focus on elements central to workplace climate. Research from Hay Group points to the importance climate plays in business results.[3] People in positive work environments outperform those who work in negative climates by 10 to 30 percent. In a positive work environment, people are more confident about their work. They enjoy working with one another. As in the party analogy, it's the people who make the difference between a fun party and a dud. In the workplace, who has the greatest influence on the climate? According to Hay Group's research, it's the immediate leader—you. You set the mood in the work environment. In fact, your leadership style impacts climate by up to 70 percent.[4]

Think about that 70 percent. It's mostly how you show up and interact with others that shapes the climate that influences your team's performance. For instance, consider these leadership styles:

* *Welcoming.* Do you have a range of conversation types with your employees?

* *Curious.* Do you inquire into how things are going on their projects? Into their personal lives?

* *Social.* How often do you connect them to others within the organization that might help them achieve their goals?

* *Thoughtful.* How frequently do you coach your employees to develop resilience in a demanding work environment?

It's the words you use and the tone of your interactions with your team that influence climate. Purpose influences climate. Stringer and Litwin explain that clear role definitions help to positively shape climate.[5] High performance expectations are also essential. Autonomy shapes climate. Trust and a sense of belonging are also key to a positive work environment. These are all elements within your control. This is what makes climate a powerful influence.

From a leadership perspective, climate is easier to influence than culture and is useful in creating lasting change necessary for the organization to create value. Culture is embedded deep into the bedrock of the organization and is hard to change. It *can* take years to shift culture.

Through your leadership style, you can shape the climate to positively influence how team members perceive, experience, and respond to work.

For positive workplaces to thrive, leaders must get to know the whole employee. Not only is this a fundamental belief that's important to optimistic workplaces, it also requires a fundamental shift in thinking about your leadership style. Today you need to be relatable—you need to be more human. Also critical to shifting the climate is to demonstrate that you care about each person's well-being: Do your employees have a healthy mix between their work lives and personal lives? The former leadership style of command and control has little relevance in the modern workplace.

> *For positive workplaces to thrive, leaders must get to know the whole employee.*

TRANSFORMED WORK EXPERIENCE

It's 8:00 a.m., and the first wave of people arrive at work. They shuffle their way to cubes and offices ready to do their work for the day. The next time this daily ritual happens, notice how it unfolds. Observe what people's body language signals. Are they interacting with one another? Every person arriving at work is bringing with him the world he left behind and carries forward the anticipation of what the day holds for him. But there is more to this seemingly mundane ritual. If you look deeper, you'll see on the faces how employees feel about the day. It's in their arrival that you can check the pulse of what the work environment's influence is and how it affects people. Is there anticipation? Eagerness? Or does body language signal something less motivating?

Between the endless offerings of meetings and the occasional break, the day is consumed by the needs of others and pressing deadlines. With this reality, it can be hard to imagine an aspirational tone making its mark on the workplace. How could it? After all, there is work to be done and no time for activities and interactions other than meetings and the work squeezed in between. This, though, is where the logic breaks down. The belief that there is no time for the leadership activities and interactions that yield optimism is as outdated as viewing employees as assets or resources.

In a 2014 study by LinkedIn of 18,000 employees, 15 percent were satisfied with their jobs and didn't want to leave. Research by Gallup from the same year found 13 percent of people were engaged with their work.[6] There's not much hope in those numbers. Pair these abysmally low numbers with the aspirations of employees and you can see that a desire for a better work climate lurks, but in most organizations there's not much opportunity for it to emerge.

In a report from Net Impact, 58 percent of students identified with the importance of working for an organization that aligns with their values. In the same study, 54 percent said they believe it's important to them to make a difference for others. Ninety-one percent of students— the future workforce—want a positive culture where they work. In the same study, 88 percent of all workers wanted the same thing.[7] These numbers reflect the aspirations of today's workforce. What is being done about it in your organization?

Too many leaders are waiting for someone else to start the work to improve the culture or the climate. Certainly it is ideal to have a top-down approach to improving both. Yet today's senior leaders are not effectively addressing people-related business concerns. In a Towers Watson study, fewer than half of the respondents agreed that their organization's senior leaders were sincerely interested in their employees' well-being.[8] How it feels to work in your team and within the organization is a critical workforce development issue. We need more leaders who are willing to choose to set a positive tone for their teams despite what senior management isn't doing. This can be done by intentionally leveraging the nuances and interplay between what I call the Origins of Optimism. I'll explain this a little later in this chapter. Will you choose to create a positive work experience even if your organization isn't focusing on it?

WORKPLACE OPTIMISM

What is workplace optimism? If you think it's viewing the proverbial glass half full through rose-colored glasses and thinking positive thoughts, you're mistaken. It is more than a positive attitude. Workplace optimism shapes attitudes. It shapes a person's and even a team's spirit. It is the spark that fuels esprit de corps. It evokes positive emotions in team members toward their work and others. Workplace optimism is a characteristic of climate. The climate feels optimistic. People are inspired by their work and the possibilities inherent in it. Workplace optimism is the belief that good things will come from hard work.

Research shows that you can transform the work experience by focusing on the best positive potential realities.[9] Rather than spend time focusing on what's wrong or missing in the workplace, you can choose to focus on what's right and possible in the workplace. Rather than ignoring the climate, you can observe how it's influencing work quality and relationships. You can transform the work experience by simply recognizing and leveraging human nature.

Today, leaders need to recognize the impact work has on people's overall life satisfaction. It is an antiquated belief that leaders should focus solely on the professional side of team members' lives. Work needs to be a positive influence, given that it consumes much of our waking time. The work we do and how we feel about it shapes our identity. Leaders have a responsibility to help their teams understand the importance of their work.

Workplace optimism is not a touchy-feely organizational theory that ignores the need for profitability or the downsides of work life. Workplaces flourish because a team's good work yields superior business outcomes. The work experience is transformed by the motivating nature of optimism. Consider the success of Barry-Wehmiller.

> *Workplace optimism is the belief that good things will come from hard work.*

Bob Chapman, CEO of Barry-Wehmiller, a $1.7 billion international capital equipment manufacturing company, doesn't talk about what his company does. He tells stories about the people in his organization.[10] "Business could be the most powerful force for good if it embraces the responsibility and impact [it] makes on people's lives," Chapman explains passionately.[11]

While Barry-Wehmiller is also successful by traditional business measures, Chapman is eager to shift away from a sole focus on profit: "It's about taking your people to a better place where they can express their gifts; they can have personal growth; they can go home fulfilled, and they can inspire their kids."[12] Chapman's focus on ensuring that the work environment positively influences his people's personal lives is how he shapes an optimistic workplace. By bringing together a business's need to create value and by caring deeply for his people, Chapman found a winning mix for performance and success. He believes so strongly in people that the company's tagline is "Building great people is our business."

THE SUN ALSO RISES IN THE EAST

Defying stereotypes of Chinese businesses, Alibaba, the site that brings together consumers, merchants, and third-party service providers to sell products to customers around the world, has carved out an optimistic climate for its employees.[13] The company's CEO, Jack Ma, is known to appeal to people's aspirations for doing good in the world and not just making a quick buck. While Alibaba's climate has been characterized as intense, employees are loyal, self-motivated, and cheerful. Ma's leadership style is strategic in nature, as is evidenced by how clear the company's mission is to employees.[14] In one report from Forbes.com, employees are said to always have the company on their minds.[15]

Ma's style is also relatable. He's known for spending time with employees to understand their needs and help them feel welcome and wanted. To promote freedom, Ma had all the punch clocks removed, a stellar example of mirroring the climate to cultural practices.[16] In another example showing Ma's ability to relate to people, he said at a company event, "People don't believe in dreams anymore. A lot of young people. And we want to tell them it's the dreams you have to keep."[17] Ma's ability to relate to people helps him create a climate that attracts people who want to stay with the company.

While it's too early in the company's relatively short history to say how profitable Alibaba will become, Ma and his leadership team are building a strong cultural foundation. But they are also creating a climate that inspires people's loyalty and desire to do their best work.

THE OPTIMISM BELIEFS

However demotivating your climate, the good news is you can positively shift what your employees experience at work. That's what this book is intended to do: help you chart a path forward to create optimism where you work. (In Appendix 1, you'll find the Optimism Planner. It's designed to bring to life in an actionable way the key concepts presented in this book.) You can position employees to believe that work is a bright spot in their life. It will take changing some outdated beliefs about your role and your team's role. In my work with leaders over the years, the following beliefs emerged as essential to helping create a positive work experience:

1. The Team Is More Important Than Any Individual

Alice was unaware of how her need to look good, be right, and be creative at all costs was undermining her team's performance. As a senior leader for a Fortune 100 company, Alice was overusing her strengths and talents so she could shine. Because she cast a long shadow, her team grumbled daily about Alice's need to be in the limelight. She took for granted her team's hard work. Rather than focus her attention on activities appropriate for a senior manager, she interfered with her team's efforts when she found their work interesting. Her involvement caused rework or slowed progress. The team thought her meddling was inappropriate, even unprofessional.

Alice epitomizes the traditional approach to work: Do your best so you look good. The main problem with this approach is it undermines the team's overall performance. How is the team's performance influenced? Matthew Lieberman, an award-winning professor at UCLA and acclaimed authority in the field of social neuroscience, has an insightful explanation. Lieberman explains in his book *Social: Why Our Brains Are Wired to Connect* that our brains are wired to be social and to find connection with others. But that's not the insightful part; our ancestors needed to be social and connect with others to survive. What is insightful is Lieberman's observation that we continually make sense of our world by evaluating our relationships with others. The more social we are, the more satisfied we feel. Our brains are wired to think about the thoughts, feelings, and goals of other people. This is called the default network. Lieberman explains that the default network automatically turns on when we aren't doing other activities. In those downtimes, our brains begin to think about other people and our relationship to them.[18] We are hardwired to be social, to develop relationships and maintain them.

Though Alice's team felt connected to each other, they didn't feel connected to her. Their ability to be social with her was hindered by their dissatisfaction with her leadership. They were angry, frustrated, and tired from her need to look good. Alice had failed to create an environment that fostered connectivity and a deeper relationship with her. As a consequence of her leadership style and the edgy climate, Alice's team's performance was capped.

The chaos Alice's poor leadership created was a distraction from developing a cohesive team identity. When a team can move together as a unified group to achieve desired outcomes, it helps create a positive environment. The rugged individuals like Alice undermine such a positive climate and, consequently, desired results.

Does individual performance still count? Absolutely. Each person must contribute his best talents. Organizations have grown too familiar with relying on the usual suspects, the same people to do high-profile projects. The problem with this is it reinforces the practice of looking out for one's own success and interests. For optimism to be strong, a cohesive team is vital. People need to believe the team will be there for them when needed. A team is weakened when the first priority is the needs of each person, or when ego dictates a team's actions or inaction.

2. There's Value to Experiencing Joy at Work

The merits of joy at work are a growing focus in organizational life. Researcher and psychologist Barbara Fredrickson has discovered that the value of joy goes beyond the hedonism of feeling good. Fredrickson found that the positive emotion of joy helps broaden what she calls our thought-action repertoires.[19] This is when our brain, in a positive state, can identify more ways to respond to circumstances compared to the effects of negative emotions. The latter has a narrowing effect on our ability to determine how to respond to social interactions and situations. When our brains are opened by positive emotions like joy, we can better see connections and more options to solve work problems.

Going a step further, joy can positively shape the work environment.[20] The emotion of joy can elicit positive action in those who feel it. Causally, how one feels affects one's actions. In the context of work, when joy is commonly expressed, it can create a safe environment and positively shape how one feels about the workplace.

What does all this mean in a work context? When people feel that the work environment is safe, optimistic, and yes, joyful, they are more likely to contribute their best. Quite simply it feels good when you're doing your best work.

As it turns out, joy isn't just about finding happiness, but also about playing; play at work is useful when creativity and innovation are needed. The usefulness of creativity and innovation to the workplace is linked to increasing employees' knowledge and skills.[21] Play at work can be doing work that energizes you. It means having friends at work and experiencing work-life mix and sharing personal moments.

Menlo Innovations can sustain its growth by focusing on creating joy for its customers and consequently make *Inc.* magazine's fastest-growing U.S. companies list multiple times. A focus on joy has created tangible business results for Menlo Innovations. Since the publication of Menlo Innovations CEO Rich Sheridan's book, *Joy, Inc.,* the company has seen a 20 percent increase in visits to its headquarters in Ann Arbor, Michigan.[22] Tours of the Menlo Software Factory accounted for approximately 10 percent of Menlo's annual revenue in 2014. Second-quarter revenues for Menlo in 2014 were up 20 percent compared to the same period in 2013. As further proof that business leaders believe joy has business relevance, executives from Fortune 100 and 500 companies make their way to see and learn from Menlo's joy-making philosophy.

Expressing joy is simple. Give a proud smile when a team member does great work. Go out of your way to recognize people in ways that are meaningful to them. Celebrate reaching key project milestones or momentous occasions in an employee's life—buying a new house or having a baby, for example. You simply need to practice showing joy as an emotion. It's a powerful way to strengthen the connection between you and your team.

3. Doing Good Is Good for Business

It's advantageous to make a contribution to improving your employees' lives. In business, this means leaders must adopt business practices that help employees have a personal life. Despite what your company's practice is, you can implement a policy banning team members from emailing each other about business on weekends. In our 24/7 culture, and given the ubiquity of smartphones, we habitually respond to the chime announcing a new email. Do good by not contributing to the stress levels of your employees who struggle to find a healthy mix between their personal and work lives.

Consider, for example, BambooHR. Based in Utah, the software development company has an antiworkaholic policy. The small start-up has found that when its team members have time to pursue personal interests, they are more productive and satisfied at work.

Barry-Wehmiller pays attention to the divorce rate of its associates. Why? An overwhelming workload adversely affects relationships and marriages. Trouble at home negatively impacts performance at work. A "Do Good" philosophy emphasizes doing what you can to help your employees bring their best selves to work. In this era when skepticism toward organizations and leaders runs high, "Do Good" provides a counterbalance, helping to reestablish trust and shape a positive work experience.

4. Relationships with Employees Need to Be Richer

While laissez-faire economic wisdom says each of us pursuing our rational self-interests will create better results, new research shows the opposite. In fact, researchers looking to understand cooperative behavior found that 30 percent of people behaved as if selfishly, and 50 percent of people behaved cooperatively. According to the research the remaining 20 percent behaved unpredictably, choosing to cooperate, or not, or refusing to do anything. Studies have found neural pathways that are inclined toward cooperation; we're hardwired for it.[23]

Relationships are central to it as well. Conventional wisdom says that by working together we can accomplish greater, more desirable outcomes. Take, for example, the remarkable 2014 events at Market Basket, a 73-store grocery chain based in Massachusetts owned by the Demoulas family.

Cousins Arthur T. Demoulas and Arthur S. Demoulas battled over who would run the business. In a typical corporate maneuver, Arthur S. successfully persuaded the board to fire the beloved Arthur T. The motive? More money for the family shareholders. Reportedly the board was unhappy about a series of bad investments that amounted to large losses and shareholders received small payouts. Additionally, the board had grown tired of the company's generous pay structure and pension programs. These, too, led to small shareholder dividends.[24] The change backfired, however.

Arthur T. had intentionally and genuinely taken time to know his employees beyond their roles at the stores. He celebrated personal triumphs with his employees and was there when life's lows impacted someone on the team. Arthur T.'s actions went beyond management. He was a steward, caring for those who cared for the business and customers.

The solid relationship Arthur T. had with employees ignited a passionate walkout when he was fired. Employees picketed against the store's new management. Additionally, a consumer boycott of Market Basket was a symbolic show of support for the ousted Arthur T.

What's fascinating about the boycott was the show of support by the picketing employees, who were standing up for a leader who had invested in them. Customers and suppliers joined the employees in their protest. Losing an estimated $70 million a day, Market Basket was in serious trouble.

The battle ended with Arthur T. buying the 50.5 percent of the business he didn't own from his cousin, Arthur S. With humility, Arthur T. addressed his supporters, praising them for their "enduring human spirit" and demonstrating that purpose and meaning will prevail. The show of support from employees, suppliers, and customers was the result of a collaborative effort and strong relationships.[25]

5. Work Should Align with Purpose and Meaning

In Arthur T.'s praise for his supporters, he acknowledged the importance that purpose and meaning played in the showdown with his cousin. Purpose and meaning are too often downplayed while busi-

nesses emphasize financial motivators such as salary, bonuses, and p
increases. This outdated mindset blinds too many leaders from helping
employees do work that matters.

Workplace optimism thrives when people understand why they
show up to work. Not only is the purpose and meaning of work important, but so, too, are the personal implications. Achieving this is a seis-
mic shift for many leaders. This shift requires that we reevaluate and
deepen our understanding of why team members show up to work daily.
Certainly for some it's a means to an end. For those who generate the
greatest value for the organization, their performance is driven by a
profound need to understand why their work matters and how their life
will be improved having invested their time and talents for your cause.

The opportunity costs are too great to do work that doesn't matter.
Personal expression through work is a
major contributor to your employees' well-
being. Doing work that matters facilitates
the expression of one's talents. It leads to
optimal performance for those who believe
in their purpose and find meaning in their
work and in life.

> *A focus on financial
> motivators blinds leaders
> from helping employees do
> work that matters.*

6. Leaders Need to Actualize Human Potential

You will learn about Luck Companies in Chapter 3. For now I want to
draw attention to its belief in human potential. Luck Companies believes
that "all human beings have the extraordinary potential to make a positive difference in the world."[26] For Luck, this foundational belief shapes
how its leaders treat one another, develop their associates, and intentionally spread the message globally.

Actualizing human potential is built on the fundamental belief that
people are inherently good, will do good, and can be trusted. Leadership
expert Douglas McGregor has advocated this perspective for decades.
We must move beyond advocation and evolve to action. Throughout this
book, I will show you ways to actualize your people's potential. These
methods are central to causing the emergence of workplace optimism.
Actualizing human potential puts the spirit into workplace optimism.

• • •

Each of the six beliefs serves as a guide to help you switch your workplace to be more suitable for people. They also support your efforts to achieve expected results. Whether individually or combined, examine them and how they can help make a shift in your team's climate. Also important is how the beliefs provide guidance for you as you explore what actions to take to create a positive place to work.

ORIGINS OF OPTIMISM

Optimistic climates don't follow a people-first philosophy. They don't follow a profit-first philosophy either. Instead they follow a dynamic exchange among three elements that create a motivating environment: purpose, meaningful work, and extraordinary people. I call these three elements the Origins of Optimism.

The dynamics among these three work like this: Purpose informs employees' work at the same time influencing a community of people to align with its own aspirations. The work directs what extraordinary people focus on. Simultaneously, the people influence what work needs to be done, how, and when. Both extraordinary people and the work advance the purpose.

The Origins of Optimism—purpose, meaningful work, and extraordinary people—interact with each other in one dynamic exchange. There is no number one. The three elements are interdependent.

For any one element to be successful, the other two need to be healthy. Remove an element, and the dynamic exchange falls apart; so, too, does the positive influence it has on the organization. Let's break down each element at a high level. I'll explain the Origins of Optimism in detail throughout the book, including how to use each element to guide your work to create the conditions for optimism. For now, however, here's a high-level breakdown of each element.

Begin with Purpose

Purpose is the passionate drive for a cause that unites the heads, hearts, hands, and guts of your people. It's a prime motivator. In one study, 77 percent of millennials indicated that a company's purpose is part of the reason they work there.[27] What's unique in optimistic climates is how purpose extends to individuals, too. In optimistic climates, team members' own purpose outside of work is encouraged. Leaders who create positive work environments expect their people to explore their purpose. It's not necessarily a spiritual expectation, but a logical one.

Employees who are personally fulfilled are more likely to seek fulfillment in their profession. Deloitte, a global management consultancy and Fortune 100 company, believes in the business value of purpose. It views purpose as the reason managers and other employees come to work each day. In a Deloitte survey, 66 percent of respondents from companies who don't believe purpose is clear don't have a history of meeting financial performance expectations. In contrast, 91 percent of organizations with a strong sense of purpose do satisfy stakeholders by meeting financial performance expectations.[28]

How do you know if your employees are clear on the organization's purpose? Check their ability to synchronize their role to why the team exists. More obvious than that, however, is their enthusiasm. Purpose lights people up. There's an aliveness within people who have purpose, who work with purpose, who align with a purpose. When I ask employees at organizations about the role purpose plays in their work, answers go beyond the tactical. There is a red thread of understood significance between their efforts and the outcomes they create. Employees aren't satisfied to show up and do eight hours of work when a vibe of optimism thrives. They expect to make a difference. Here are some statements from employees I have interviewed about how purpose helps them in their work:

* "[My purpose is to] help customers achieve greater levels of success."

* "It sets people free to do great work."

* "It makes lives better."

* "Creates an environment to let innovation flourish."

* "Be a safe harbor [for people]."

* "Help people reach their goals."

* "Give information in a helpful manner so that it's understood."

* "Be an advocate and adviser for the customer."

What stands out in these statements and the many others from my research is how selfless the statements are. Notice that the value from purpose is centered on supporting others and is a reason for doing the work. Purpose may be altruistic in nature, but its ability to unify a group of people is essential for organizations that want to stand apart from their competition. Going a step further, team members who share a sense of purpose are more willing to support one another through the grind of work and celebrate victories together. Teams that lack a sense of shared purpose don't take time to celebrate key accomplishments. I explore the importance of purpose and its role personally and organizationally in depth in Chapter 6.

Make Work Meaningful

The difference between work and meaningful work is the influence it has on the person. Meaningful work has significance. The reasons for doing it matter and expand a person's potential. Work without meaning is merely something to cross off a to-do list. There is little productive emotional investment in the work. Rather than contribute to employee growth, work without meaning drains and stagnates employee potential. In Chapter 7 I'll explain how to create the conditions for your team members to find meaning in their work. Notice I say "create the conditions." Ultimately, it is up to each person to determine what is meaningful work. Yet what is powerful about climate is that you can influence it through workplace optimism.

A study from McKinsey & Company identified a *meaning quotient* as the key category for peak performance. Susie Cranston and Scott Keller of McKinsey & Company explain the meaning quotient as a peak performance experience where individuals believe the work they do matters and is also a new attempt at solving a business problem. A low meaning quotient, according to Cranston and Keller, means employees invest little energy in the job and see it merely as a means to an end.[29]

Joanna Barsh, who is an author and a McKinsey director, has spent over 10 years researching what she calls centered leadership. Meaning is a dimension of it and was five times more influential on work satisfaction than other dimensions in her research.[30] Research from Ken Blanchard Companies found that meaningful work was the top choice nearly 40 percent of the time when people ranked important job factors.[31]

We all want meaning in our lives, both personally and professionally. Meaning, like purpose, is a leadership focus with the intention to support team members' pursuit of it in all arenas of their lives.

Attract Extraordinary People

The final element to the Origins of Optimism is people. This element is about aligning a community of people—your team—to a shared purpose. It's still a leader's responsibility to learn what motivates each person on her team. The nuance is that people aren't singled out as the primary focus. It's the community of people that grabs the leader's attention. Care for the whole and nurture the individual. This is what helps foster an optimistic workplace.

In a positive climate, people are believed to be and treated as mature, fully functioning adults. This is an important perspective for Netflix, the online television network.

There's a saying at Netflix that it hires "fully formed adults." Aligning with this belief are policies—or an absence of policies—that give employees freedom that assumes they will act in the best interests of the company. For example, expense reports aren't required, and employees have unlimited vacation time.[32] It isn't readily known if the absence of a vacation policy at Netflix leads to employees acting in the best interests of the company. However, with high-profile companies like Richard Branson's Virgin Group and the Internet company Evernote adopting a similar vacation philosophy, the business value is catching on within forward-thinking organizations. But there is more to this than business value. Building an organi-

> *Care for the whole and nurture the individual. This is what helps foster an optimistic workplace.*

zation on the fundamental belief that employees can be trusted and treated like fully functioning, mature adults is common sense. It's also an essential input for creating a positive work environment.

You may not have the authority or influence to change policies related to expenses and vacations. Instead, you can focus on where you can give employees more freedom to demonstrate your belief in their maturity and ability to show up as fully functioning adults. People do rise to the occasion when they are trusted and high expectations are the norm.

Netflix has created an environment that helps a community of people work together. They believe strongly in "[helping] each other be great."[33] When is the next time you will communicate this expectation to your team in such simple, clear language?

You are not a babysitter scrutinizing your team's work. That is an outdated perspective attributed to management. Nowadays leaders are expected to continuously develop a self-awareness about how their actions and words influence others. Netflix considers this a characteristic of what it calls "The Rare Responsible Person." Such a person is self-motivated, self-disciplined, and proactive in his actions; he acts because it's the right thing to do.[34] Is this person rare? I don't believe so. They may be hidden because the climate has not made people feel safe to stick one's neck out and stand up for one's beliefs or big ideas. People want to do the right thing. They want to care about their work. They need, however, an environment that rewards such behaviors.

Attracting extraordinary people to your team is easiest when team members feel there is a sense of relatedness among them. Relatedness emerges when team members help each other be great and do their share of work without being asked. As a result, rewarding relationships flourish. This adds enjoyment and brings well-being to the workplace.

The people element of the Origins of Optimism is essential to foster a strong, cohesive group that can adapt to the changes demanded of the team or the organization's purpose. In these environments, people need to be able to pivot their focus quickly when work changes or as purpose evolves.

WHAT ABOUT PROFIT?

Profit is noticeably absent from the trio of elements outlined here that includes purpose, meaningful work, and extraordinary people. That's not due to a lack of importance. Profit isn't listed because profit doesn't directly contribute to the workplace environment—the way it feels. Sure, profit helps contribute to important physical elements in the work environment. However, profit is an outcome from the purpose-driven work and from the high-performing workforce that wholly invests its strengths and talents for the good of the organization.

Another reason I've not included profit as part of the Origins of Optimism is due to the growing awareness that profit is no longer the primary marker of organizational success. In a 2012 Deloitte study, one measure of business success found that 76 percent of leaders said they believed the value of a business should be measured by its impact on society as well as its profits. Forty-four percent said they believe profit margin is the primary success determinant. And in a third measure, 71 percent of leaders disagreed with profit margin being the primary success measure.[35]

The growing trend away from profit as a sole measure of success is in part due to the millennial mindset. Rather than pin the shift in attitudes on one generation, people of all ages are advocating for something more than the myopic perspective on profit. Purpose, societal impact, and profit together are what today's employees and a growing number of company leaders advocate for measures of success.

WHY WORKPLACE OPTIMISM?

The garage at Luck Companies is full of big rock-crushing equipment. Tires stand tall at seven feet on some. As in most garages, the smell is a mixture of oil and dirt. With a deliberate stride, Kelly comes up and shakes my hand. Kelly is one of the mechanics. He's a quiet, friendly man. Kelly agreed to be interviewed for this book. "I'm not sure what I can add," he says to me. But once he starts talking about the influence Luck has had on his life, words flow.

Like many in organizations around the world, Kelly didn't expect much from his employer. Though he had heard great things about the company, he had no idea how his life would become so satisfying. It's those last six words that hold the answer to the question of why you should focus on workplace optimism. The influence optimism has on a company's people goes beyond the confines of the office space. Workplace optimism contributes to everyone's overall life satisfaction. This theme surfaced again and again in the interviews I have had with team members in companies of all sizes. A work environment that inspires hope and ignites people's potential has a positive influence on employees' personal life.

Kelly said to me that he "can go home stress-free" because of the climate in his work team. He told me a story about the time a company executive wanted to learn the business by working at the garage. In place of talking with Kelly about the job requirements, the executive scooted under one of the machines with him and asked to be put to work. The show of support made Kelly feel valued and immediately built rapport between the two men. In exchange for "stress-free" and respect, Kelly goes out of his way to do his best.

It's the leader's responsibility to create an environment that motivates. The benefits Kelly receives from work and the extra effort he puts into it are just two reasons for leaders to focus on creating an optimistic climate. There is, though, a more logical one: It's good for business.

In the 10 years since Luck Companies has rolled out its values-based leadership philosophy to all its associates across all lines of business, the aggregate company has seen tremendous results. While the company keeps much of its financial details private, it shared some financial metrics with me to help show how an optimistic workplace has been beneficial.

> *It's the leader's responsibility to create an environment that motivates people to do their best work.*

From 2004 through 2014, Luck increased by 25 percent revenue generated per labor dollar expensed. Leading its industry competitors, its gross profit per ton of stone was up 81 percent in the same 10-year period. Average profitability as a percentage of net sales is about 16 percent higher than the average profitability margin of the company's two main competitors. Even customers see the benefits from values-based leadership on the climate. Luck's net promoter score, which measures the likelihood that a customer will promote a business to others, is in the 78 to 83 percent range. Anything above 50 percent is considered excellent. It's considered an important metric when measuring how effective the service is from the customer's perspective.[36]

Workplace optimism is simply a place to start to make a difference for your people and for the business. It's a leadership opportunity that can turn work into a contribution to people's lives. Additionally, it can positively shape how people view and experience working on your team or in your company. Certainly there are other options to achieve results like those Kelly told me. The key is to choose to act.

You've now read the central elements to an optimistic climate, but what exactly does it look like? Here's what it looks like when it takes root and positively transforms the work environment:[37]

1. People anticipate good things will come from their work.

2. Personal and professional goals are achieved.

3. Personal and professional worlds are integrated.

4. People make satisfying progress with their work.

5. Financial metrics are achieved.

6. People are viewed as significant and the heart of success.

7. Values-based leadership guides actions and decisions.

8. Partnership and collaboration replaces hierarchy-driven interactions.

9. Community building is encouraged.

10. Organizational and personal purpose guide decisions.

11. Strengths are maximized.

Keep in mind that the vibe in your team is constantly changing. So the conditions listed above may not all be present at the same time. That's okay. What you choose to focus on based on the needs of your team will influence heavily what emerges as important.

The above conditions create a picture of a better way to work. Creating workplace optimism is about leveraging what human beings want in life and infusing that into the way you lead and connect with others.

Not all leaders will choose to improve the climate of the workplace. That's okay. You see the opportunities. The benefits far outweigh the costs and toll that a negative environment has on people.

We spend the majority of our time interacting with others at work. In light of this reality, it's merely common sense that we invest the time and exert the energy to overhaul how we work together, define value from our efforts, and create and find meaning in where we chose to invest our time.

CHAPTER 2

Destructive Management

Our attention becomes fixated on those at the top. We live the myth that if you do not have sponsorship from the top, you cannot realize your intentions.
—PETER BLOCK, *STEWARDSHIP*

SYMPTOMS OF DESTRUCTIVE MANAGEMENT

Destructive management is really a collection of symptoms of ill-fitting practices for the modern workplace. They result from misjudged or uninformed choices. Mostly the symptoms present themselves when a steward doesn't shift along with the demands of today's workforce and workplace expectations.

Their impacts on people and the organization vary, depending on the length the symptoms go unaddressed. If you think of destructive management like a disease, people and the organization can't perform at their peak potential. Both are often distressed. Along with distress, a host of unpleasant outcomes dominate people's experiences. Recovery from problems is slow. In severe cases, people just can't seem to shake the feeling that things just won't get better. The negative feeling of the workplace is alienating. Optimism is choked before it can even emerge.

Ultimately, the impacts from destructive management can be traced back to six symptoms:

Symptom 1: Blind Impact

A leader who is unaware of how her actions, attitude, and words impact others and results damages any opportunity for workplace optimism. Going a step further, blind impact is a result of misusing the power of influence a leader has in having a positive impact on those with whom she interacts. She is unaware of the motivating importance of purpose, organizationally and personally. She doesn't consistently develop people or herself, as the value is underestimated. Often this symptom prevents a leader from connecting the dots between people's work and organizational direction. Blind impact can easily emerge from a lack of one-on-one meetings, or connection with others.

Symptom 2: Antisocial Leadership

This is not antisocial in the psychological sense, a dysfunction of thinking about and perceiving social situations, or relating to people.[1] Rather, I am referring to a leader's resistance to embrace social behaviors illuminated by social technology. This symptom is all about one's inability to encourage, build, and evolve a community of people united by a shared purpose.

The first example of behavior that demonstrates antisocial leadership is an autocratic style. It's easier for this type of leader to dictate what people should do. He may even distrust people. His interpersonal skills may be awkward. This person is unaware of his voice as a leader and how to use it for good.

This symptom adversely impacts the work environment by creating a void of connectedness, or relatedness. An antisocial leader doesn't stop long enough to see the value of relationships among his employees and peers. Optimism cannot emerge when antisocial beliefs and actions dominate, including an unawareness of the importance to engage with the external community where the organization does business.

The powerful uses of social technology are epitomized by people's willingness to unconditionally give back to others. On Twitter, people will help promote another person's work and ask nothing in return. In the workplace, the dynamic is obviously different, but the sentiment is the same, but not for an antisocial leader. Such a leader may blatantly take credit for another person's or group's work. He may also not see the need to give praise for the good work of others. In his book *Give and Take*, Adam Grant describes takers, in part, as people who demonstrate authority by raising their voice and using body language to assert their dominance.[2]

Taking, as a symptom of antisocial leadership, reduces the interaction between people as purely transactional. It leaves people feeling used. It has a negative impact on workplace optimism.

Symptom 3: Chronic Change Resistance

What's destructive about this symptom is the leader's unwillingness to initiate change to help her team and the organization remain relevant. The seduction of the status quo overpowers rational thoughts and actions. And if change is adopted, it's usually late in the change-adoption curve. With this leader in charge, only incremental change is possible.

Symptom 4: Profit Myopia

Another symptom of destructive management is the outdated belief that profit is the only success measure. Leaders with profit myopia are short-term focused to a fault. Their teams chase solutions that satisfy shareholders and/or short-term goals, alienating customers and employees.

Taking a chink out of the optimistic workplace is this leader's narrow focus on his own personal income and rewards. These are more important than inspiring employees. Furthermore, such a pursuit insulates the leader from realizing that other motivators beyond money are important.

Symptom 5: Constipated Inspiration

Much like blind impact, this symptom stems from a lack of awareness. The leader is unsure of how to inspire people on her team. Often she is too focused on her own needs, giving little attention to what her employees experience when at work. As a result, she doesn't see what demotivates or what inspires people. At the core of constipated inspiration is ignorance of personal values. If a leader knew what she stood for, she'd have more awareness of who she is. Consequently, she would have greater capacity for learning about the people on her team.

On an organizational level, this leader stifles innovation and creativity. Neither can exist in an uninspired environment. Both need energy to grow. There is an absence of energy when inspiration isn't in the work environment.

Symptom 6: Silo Syndrome

The final symptom of destructive management may not be the most costly, but it's quite common. Silo syndrome afflicts a leader when he cannot see beyond his immediate responsibilities. Also, silo syndrome blinds a leader from seeing the impacts of work on other people's lives.

With this symptom, a leader is unaware of or doesn't care how work life affects employees' family lives. There is no healthy mix between the two worlds. Work dominates; personal time suffers from neglect.

Also common with this syndrome is seeing people merely as a role: People in sales know nothing about marketing; customer service employees know nothing about operations. Silo syndrome is like a mental shortcut: It reduces things to their simplest form to quickly make sense of them. We don't challenge our mental shortcuts; we assume they are correct. Often the logic is spotty, and the conclusions are misinformed.

> *Workplace energy is absent when inspiration isn't present in the workplace.*

It's common to hear stories of disrespected, mistreated, and ignored employees. Simply look at the impact found in global employee engagement numbers. Or worse yet, the proliferation of passive management, the old-school type, that fails to address bad behaviors and performance that lead to mediocrity. Destructive management is made up of disruptors to optimism in the workplace. They distract you and your team from experiencing fulfillment in work and from ultimately creating the value the organization needs.

OUTDATED BELIEFS OF THE WORKPLACE

A man walks into a bar and notices another man with a big orange head. Curious, the man asks the bartender, "What's up with the guy with the big orange head?" The bartender encourages the man to buy the guy a drink and learn the story. "It's fascinating," says the bartender.

So the man sits down and listens to the guy with the big orange head and learns that he released a genie from a bottle. Naturally, the genie granted him three wishes. Predictably, he wished for wealth, and a beautiful woman to be his wife. The genie granted his wishes. "You have one wish left," the genie proclaimed.

Taking a drink from his beer, the man with the big orange head said, "This is where I may have gone wrong. I wished for a big orange head."[3]

This anti-joke may point out my quirky taste in jokes, but it also reveals something about human nature: People are prone to make poor choices. So it is with how we cling white-knuckled to how the workplace used to be. We choose to ignore the signs that what people want from their work isn't lifetime security or a boss giving commands of what to do and when and how to do it.

Just as some of us fail to make choices that lead to our growth, leaders are choosing to overlook ideas that can make a positive environment, and, instead, cling to outdated beliefs of the workplace. They're familiar, comfortable. Like the choice the man with the big orange head made, too many leaders are making poor choices by ignoring the call to action to transform the workplace climate to be positive. The impact of destructive management limits employee contribution, reduces the growth of the business, and stifles customer/client satisfaction.

Organizational theorist Douglas McGregor wrote, "It is assumed almost without question that organizational requirements take precedence over the needs of individual members."[4] McGregor's take on work life was ahead of his time. Today his viewpoint is timely and reflects the outdated belief that all employees must bifurcate their personal and professional lives. It's as if somehow personal problems evaporate the moment people arrive at work. If there is a place to begin to understand how to create optimism, it's in understanding that business needs no longer trump personal needs.

Returning to BambooHR, the individual's need for a satisfying life outside work is important to the company. In an interview with me, the company's human resources director, Cassie Whitlock, explained how she personally benefits from not putting in 10- to 12-hour days. "I go home at the end of a hard day's work, don't check email or work on projects. I spend time with my family and forget about work. I come back refreshed the next day."[5] Not only are employees refreshed when they come back to work, they're finding greater fulfillment in their lives because both their personal and professional needs are being met. BambooHR believes that employees should be able to get their day's work done in eight hours. If they can't, then something is off and warrants a discussion about what that might be.

Another outdated belief about the workplace is that autonomy is not important for rank-and-file employees. As adults, we need to feel autonomous in the way we go about living our lives and making our own decisions. In the workplace, leaders should not take for granted the importance and motivating influences of autonomy. Psychology researchers Edward Deci and Richard Ryan have studied the effects of autonomy on performance and have found numerous benefits important to individuals, and ultimately to organizations. First, when people identify with work's value and "have integrated it into their sense of self," they perform better when solving problems. They also experience positive psychological health.[6] Business psychologist and psychotherapist Douglas LaBier explains that psychological health is about having the skills to manage the triumphs and trials of life, including the use of coping skills.[7]

Continuing with Deci and Ryan's research findings, they discovered that autonomy helps equip people with the persistence needed to make behavior changes important to their performance. For leaders, this is a valuable capability in today's constantly changing business environment.

While persistence is important, people need to have the energy and vitality to complete their work. The two researchers explain vitality as self-generating energy that exhilarates and empowers.[8]

From my experience as a consultant, it's common for leaders to overlook the importance of autonomy. It's not that leaders intentionally set out to rob employees of it. The lack of focus on autonomy is merely the result of unquestioned beliefs about the role of a leader and outdated business practices designed for a twentieth-century workforce.

Key to understanding the value of autonomy is understanding the difference between intrinsic and extrinsic motivation. Autonomy is an example of an intrinsic motivator. Intrinsic motivators are generated from within a person—autonomy, meaning, and purpose are examples. In comparison, extrinsic motivators, like pay or promotions, come from outside a person. These have a shorter influence on motivation. Intrinsic motivators have a longer-lasting influence on our satisfaction and willingness to do our best work. Despite popular management belief, money is not the top performance motivator.

In a 2012 study of college students nearing graduation and of employees working, 45 percent said they would take a 15 percent pay cut for work that has a social or environmental impact; 58 percent said they would take the same pay cut to work for an organization that shared their values. Now this isn't saying money isn't important. Employees simply want more from their employer: meaning, purpose, impact, growth opportunities, development, positive culture, interesting/rewarding work, flexible work hours, or work that doesn't interfere with personal time, for example.[9] It is another outdated belief to think money is the prime motivator that leads to outstanding work.

Taylor Perkins was the first person I met when I arrived at BambooHR. Bright, helpful, and cheery, she told me that her purpose at the young company is to build connections. Perkins's perspective is an important pivot in the evolution of our workplaces. Employees want to feel a sense of relatedness at work. The notion that work is merely a place we go to Monday through Friday is another outdated belief. Work is a place where friendships and alliances are created. It's where employees can experience full-life fulfillment.

Relatedness is an intrinsic motivator necessary for well-being and shaping a positive attitude one has toward work. This is key considering that climate is perceived through how employees feel about the workplace. Employees' immediate leaders influence this feeling. Other key intrinsic motivators, according to researcher Roy Baumeister, are frequent and satisfying interactions with colleagues. Baumeister also highlights the fact that caring and concern need to be characteristics of colleague interactions. Though each employee interprets the experience of relatedness, it's the steward's responsibility to shape the context for it to even be possible.[10]

The absence of relatedness at work is an important reality that needs a steward's focus. Without relatedness, your team's sense of well-being is negatively impacted. This affects the members' drive for excellence. The desire to stay is also negatively impacted. Furthermore, a lack of relatedness undermines the social fabric that knits together the interactions of those in and outside your team.

A need to feel a sense of relatedness, or belonging, is fundamental to the human condition. Survival of the human species has taught us that we can accomplish more together. This is certainly true in modern workplaces.

As a steward, your ability to accomplish your work is facilitated through relatedness. When you need resources or favors, healthy relationships are key. Without them you're limited to what you can accomplish or how far you can take your goals.

Relatedness and belonging are both centered on the need to be included as part of a group. New research has found that when a sense of belonging is absent, that situation has far worse effects on people than being bullied. To ignore someone is to deny feeling related to the group, leaving many with the sense of not being socially worthy or worth attention. It's like social death.[11] And this cuts deep.

Ostracizing others denies them the ability to be part of the social fabric that is fundamental to our existence, to our survival. In the workplace, this can take on the form of ignoring the new person on the team, or habitually ignoring the contrarian's perspective. For employees to feel as if they are part of a group, stewards need to intentionally integrate people into the team and connect team members to others throughout the organization.

Perhaps the biggest outdated belief interfering with your creating an optimistic climate is negating the importance of employees' psychological well-being.

Carol Ryff has devoted her life's work to help us understand how our psychological well-being can enrich our lives. Ryff teaches in the psychology department at The Pennsylvania State University and is director of the Institute of Aging. Her work serves as another foundational element to workplace optimism and reminds us that no matter our role at work, we all need a sense of well-being. By some estimates, we spend up to a third of our waking time in work.[12]

Psychological well-being, as Ryff defines it, has six distinct aspects. Let's continue to explore the theme that stewards can turn to fundamental human needs to transform the work experience. I've addressed two of the six items above: autonomy and relatedness. Let's look at the other four: self-acceptance, environmental mastery, purpose in life, and personal growth.

❏ *Self-Acceptance.* Ryff explains that self-acceptance, along with the other elements, are key to positive functioning as adults. In the workplace, this is about having a positive attitude toward oneself. What we miss as stewards is how our actions—such as coaching and mentoring—can and must help employees learn how to view themselves positively. This represents a significant shift in how many leaders view their role. Leaders today need to do less controlling and focus more on helping their people self-actualize through the pursuit of doing meaningful work.

❏ *Environmental Mastery.* Just as it is your responsibility to be a context shaper, each of your employees, and you, must shape the environment to meet their needs. When the work environment stops meeting our needs, our well-being can be adversely affected. Performance suffers. Clarity is murky. Relationships strain. As a leader, you have the dual role of shaping the environment to help your employees' psychological well-being and ensuring it supports yours as well.

> *Leaders need to do less controlling and focus more on helping their people self-actualize.*

❏ *Purpose in Life.* The need to live a life intentionally and with direction is not limited to what we do outside work. The effects of the destructive management can be mitigated if purpose is used more often to guide decisions. Purpose is your *why*: Why are we doing this? How does this support our mission? How does this support your personal goals?

❏ *Personal Growth.* It's important for employees to believe that their time working with you and others will help them grow in meaningful ways important to their professional and personal goals. People need to believe that personal growth is possible and is a choice available to them.

With a white-knuckled grip on the familiar ways of work, we over-look the importance psychological well-being plays in creating a positive work experience. Equally as important, without psychological well-being, we don't see our purpose as stewards to shape workplace optimism. Carol Ryff's work serves as a call to action for workplace optimism. My goal is for you to improve your team members' psychological well-being to help create workplace optimism.

The myriad outdated beliefs presented in this section have one thing in common: a misunderstanding of human needs. The practices that make up the science of management have been well honed over the last several hundred years. These practices were built on a flawed assumption—that the singular focus for running a business is what's important for the organization. Too little consideration was given to what's important for the individuals doing the work. A 2014 study by The Jensen Group on the future of work stresses the latter point. They boldly explain that our understanding of management is horribly one-sided, using "too much of a corporate-centric lens." Instead the study asserts that leadership is about a mutually beneficial relationship—what's good for the organization *and* the employee.[13] To understand this expanded viewpoint, stewards need to be insatiably curious about human needs and how to satisfy them through work.

MINDSET

Before we look at what you can do to counter destructive management and shift your beliefs about your role as a steward, let's examine the mindset necessary to confront those beliefs. To start, what comes to mind about your ability to create workplace optimism? What words or phrases would you use to describe attempting it? "Impossible"? "Who am I kidding"? "I can't do this; they don't pay me enough"? Or perhaps you think to yourself, "This will be tough, but it's worth the effort." "It's important work; I need to figure this out."

I ask you these questions to reveal how you might view yourself in terms of cultivating workplace optimism. Your answer will make a difference in your outcomes.

In her book *Mindset*, Carol Dweck explains the difference between people who have a fixed or a growth mindset. A person with a fixed mindset—the belief that people are born with a set of skills that are fixed, unchanging—may never start the work to create a positive environment. A person with a fixed mindset avoids challenges and deems them not worth taking if he doesn't believe he already has the leadership skills to do it. From her research, Dweck has learned that we can change our mindset beginning with awareness of how we see and interpret the world.

If you have a growth mindset, you believe hard work can lead to improvement. In fact, a person with a growth mindset believes it's essential to put forward the effort to master the skills to create workplace optimism.[14]

It is your choice, however, to determine the mindset necessary to shape the context that supports people in doing their best work. The reality in creating and sustaining a great place to work takes effort; it takes a growth mindset. Employees will question your intentions. You will need to stretch yourself. Your peers will warn against the dangers of getting your team's hopes up. The status quo will want you to enforce it. Others will be threatened. But you can approach overcoming the barriers to optimism by adopting a growth mindset. A leader with a growth mindset believes that:

* Skills come from hard work and can always be improved.

* Human potential is unlimited.

* Effort is required to expand knowledge and accomplish goals.

* Challenges are growth opportunities.

* Feedback from the team and peers is necessary for your growth.

* Setbacks should be anticipated and used to help make decisions in the future; one should be adaptable to change.[15]

I've made multiple claims about the choice and the difficulty inherent in creating workplace optimism. It may not be difficult for you and where you work. What is most important in this vital leadership challenge is that you choose the growth mindset. A growth mindset will strengthen you when you face obstacles and enhance your excitement when you and your team achieve your goals, or when you fail from a mistake and learn quickly what to do differently next time.

DESTRUCTIVE MANAGEMENT IMPACTS

What are the outcomes from destructive management that have a choke hold on the workplace? Certainly they vary from organization to organization. The following list includes some of the biggies. The list reflects the costs of working for an organization or in a team where outcomes from bad management have gone unaddressed and removed optimism as a possibility.

1. *Unsatisfying Home Life.* The stress from working long hours and the expectation of having to do so often result in distractedness when at home, disrupting harmony and separation from work life.

2. *Distress.* Instead of benefiting from good stress, or eustress, employees at all levels experience burnout, physical ailments, even fatigue. The influence of eustress is biological as well as mental and ultimately impacts our performance inside and outside of work. With eustress a person can cope effectively with the pressures of stress.

3. *Apathy.* The lack of interest or concern employees feel toward the meaning of work or the impact they can have.

4. *Dysfunctional Relationships.* The feeling of belonging diminishes as people don't experience connection in their interactions with team members and executives.

5. *Broken Trust.* Disbelief in what the business stands for and the intentions, actions, and words of others are pervasive. Employees at all levels question intentions and decisions, which strains relationships and adversely impacts progress in work.

6. *Unclear Goals and Priorities.* Because of short-term thinking, and in some cases a dysfunctional need to please shareholders, a company may change strategic or operational directions with little explanation of why, leaving people uncertain of the value of their effort. Progress in work slows down, and engagement and hope diminish.

7. *Scarcity of Loyalty.* This is not a millennial stereotype but a workforce trend stemming from disbelief in the good the company does for its employees and those whom they serve.

The outcomes from destructive management are too easily dismissed as workplace realities. They are viewed by traditional managers as necessary outcomes of the pursuit of profit and efficiencies. These realities fester and create a work environment that diminishes people and their ability to apply their strengths and talents to their work. However, as stewards, we can no longer overlook the costs of bad management decisions. A competitive advantage is created by the proactive steward who decides to create workplace optimism in response to the realities of today's uninspired workplaces.

GALLANT ACTS

Certainly bad management decisions cannot be avoided. A decision is better than none at all if progress is to be experienced. How you help your team through the impacts of a bad decision matters most. The outcomes of bad management are and will be a reality as long as humans are involved. We're messy and imperfect.

If you are to move past the adverse effects of some decisions and create workplace optimism, you will need to face reality as it is and take action to move your team closer to optimism. You'll need to assess where you believe your team is regarding impacts of bad management realities. The Optimism Planner in Appendix 1 will help you determine where you might want to focus your efforts to counter the effects of destructive management. For now, here are some leadership actions you can take to set you and your team down the path to the optimistic workplace:

* Bring your team together and demonstrate that you understand how the team has been negatively impacted by management decisions. Be prepared to give specific examples of what you've observed and the impacts. Be prepared to listen. Do not offer excuses. Do not blame management. As Stephen Covey advocates, "Seek first to understand, then to be understood."[16] Say that you want to shift the workplace environment to one that is positive. You will need to share your vision repeatedly.

* Meet one-on-one with members of your team and learn what's important to them in terms of the workplace. Continue to

meet with team members to show you mean business in terms of creating a positive climate. You cannot let too many distractions interfere with scheduling the one-on-ones. Occasionally postponing them is fine. But a habit of postponing them works against your vision and your intentions.

* In your one-on-ones, ask each team member what goals—personal and professional—you can support. Inspire hope that the goals are possible by helping them break the goals down into smaller ones.[17]

* As you continue to discuss what a positive work experience means with individuals and with the team, begin to talk as a group about what the team can do to support the goal of working in an optimistic workplace.

* Strengthen your social leadership by building relationships with peers across the organization. The goal here is to break down silos. Relationships help broaden your understanding of the business. You'll begin to see potential impacts when you know what's happening outside your team.

* Reduce the effects of blind impact by exploring what your team's purpose is. As that becomes clearer, ask yourself, "What does this mean to me? What's my role in this? What's my purpose?"

* Overcome constipated inspiration by learning what motivates each person on your team to excel. You want to learn this to tailor how you motivate each person in a meaningful way.

* Participate in a 360-degree assessment. The goal is to learn how your leadership style positively and negatively influences people.

CREATING POSITIVE OUTCOMES

Thomas Teal, former senior editor of the *Harvard Business Review,* explained in an article that managers need to accept the "business consequences of [the] company's acts" and "[take] personal responsibility" for them.[18] Doing this signals that the manager is beginning her transformation into a steward for both the company and her people's potential and their well-being.

Your most likely foes in accepting the reality Teal writes about are ego and/or frustration. You may think to yourself, "I can't show weakness by apologizing. I won't do it. The minute my team smells weakness, I'm through." Or perhaps you'll think, "I wasn't here when these decisions were made. Why should I shoulder the blame?" Let me address the second thought first.

Regardless of your hire date, you have a team that wants to follow you, wants to connect with you. Acknowledging how difficult decisions impacted your team is part of the process of getting past any anger, resentment, or emotional barrier to achieve workplace optimism. It also helps create or deepens the relatedness your team members can experience with you and with one another. In my interviews with employees at the model companies included in this book, I asked what advice they'd give to managers who want to create workplace optimism. Here's what they said:

* Choose first that you want to create an optimistic workplace.

* Be willing to look at yourself and decide what you need to make a positive work experience.

* Constantly think about and talk about workplace optimism.

* Believe that you create what you want the work environment to become.

* Want a better workplace.

* Get to know your employees' needs and desires.

* Shift the focus away from what you want to the benefits for the team.

* Be prepared to shield your team against other managers' negativity.

* Keep your eye on the impact you want to have on your employees' lives.

* Show a positive attitude.

✳ Show your vulnerable side by sharing what concerns and excites you about creating optimism at work.

✳ Invite the team to be part of the exploratory journey to optimism.

In terms of ego's influence on your actions as a steward, I return to the wisdom of Peter Block. He describes stewardship as the "willingness to be accountable for the well-being of the larger organization by operating in service, rather than in control, of those around us."[19] We all must work to manage the influence that ego has on our perceptions and actions.

Ego isn't bad. It can actually be useful. You need to be willing to shift how you see your responsibilities as a leader. It's not about what you will gain but how you can help others achieve success. Will you struggle? I do; so will you. This is why it's important to enroll your team in the work of creating workplace optimism. It cannot be done alone or covertly.

The positive outcomes you can co-create with your team are the same characteristics of an optimistic workplace presented in Chapter 1.

Creating optimism is a collaborative effort. You can't wait for top management to sanction a full-on transformation to workplace optimism. This is an effort that needs to start at the middle of the organization. You have the greatest influence on your team. Leverage this for maximum benefit.

CHAPTER 3

The Power of Contagious Emotions

Work is a good thing for man—a good thing for his humanity because through work man not only transforms nature, adapting it to his own needs, but he also achieves fulfillment as a human being and indeed in a sense becomes "more a human being."
—POPE JOHN PAUL II, *LABOREM EXERCENS*

PERSONAL BENEFITS AND UNPLANNED GIVING

Though the heart of this book is about creating an optimistic climate that supports your employees and shows you ways to fulfill their greatest potential, it is also about you. After all, are you not also an employee? Are you not a member of a team? You, too, deserve to have a career that helps you flourish in life, aligns with your purposes, and unlocks your potential. It's not only your team that anticipates good things from their work. I imagine you want the same, too.

On the flip side of the personal benefits are the benefits to the organization. In Chapter 1, I listed 11 benefits in which optimism transforms the work environment. Those 11 ways can be categorized into three groups: people, profit, and progress (see Table 3-1).

Table 3-1. **People, profit, and progress.**

Organizational Benefit	Workplace Optimism Benefits
People	Personal and professional goals are achieved.
	Personal and professional worlds are integrated.
	People are viewed as significant and the heart of success.
	Values-based leadership guides actions and decisions.
	Community building is encouraged.
	Strengths are maximized.
Profit	Financial metrics are achieved.
Progress	People anticipate good things will come from their work.
	People make satisfying progress with their work.
	Partnership and collaboration replaces hierarchy-driven interactions.
	Organizational and personal purpose guide decisions.

To create an optimistic workplace, stewards need a strong focus on addressing people-centric needs. As I explained in Chapter 2, meeting human needs is good for business and for employees. Benefits for the company could be increased engagement, improved retention of key people, and even higher interest from high-potential candidates in your organization. Perhaps one of the more unique benefits is unplanned giving.

Unplanned giving occurs when employees spontaneously act in ways that benefit the business that could lead to greater organizational effectiveness. A result of unplanned giving is a positive employee mood or emotion. I'd add that the spontaneity is a result of the contagiousness of the optimism in the workplace climate. Take, for example, a time when you felt good about how things were going at work. Your openness to spontaneously give of yourself to others was more likely to occur. These are the positive, spur-of-the-moment actions that catch people's attention. The contagiousness of the unplanned giving creates a virtuous cycle that pulls in more people who witness and ultimately want to mimic the mood.

Unplanned giving benefits the organization in six ways, according to professors and researchers Jennifer George and Arthur Brief. The first is demonstrated by employees helping coworkers by acting outside of their job descriptions. Second, these simple acts often go unnoticed, according to the researchers, meaning that help is given without wanting anything in return. It's done merely to support a team member. One could argue it's a selfless act. It could also be selfish.[1] Either way, employees help each other make progress in their work.

A third benefit George and Brief found is that spontaneity benefits the organization by way of protection: People look out for and report things that could harm the organization—theft or fraud, for example. Providing constructive suggestions, developing oneself, and spreading goodwill are the other benefits of unplanned giving.

Unplanned giving is unique in the sense that it occurs without prompting from the organization. It represents a genuine enthusiasm from employees for what the company does or believes. It's a powerful sign of employee engagement.[2]

The second category of organization benefit is profit. It is still an important measurement of success. It's just not the only measurement. Companies like Barry-Wehmiller, Menlo Innovations, and Luck Companies are seeing business growth as a result of their optimistic climate and people-centric beliefs and philosophies. The organization must still meet key financial targets. Without measuring and monitoring them, there would be no opportunity to create optimistic workplaces.

Finally, progress in employees' work and in key initiatives—operationally or strategically—benefits organizations by way of an engaged and satisfied workforce. Bringing a new product or service to market can only happen when there is progress in the work. Progress in the work also happens because internal processes and policies minimize or remove bureaucratic red tape, helping employees move swiftly to achieve outcomes.

But what's in it for you? What do you stand to gain by pursuing workplace optimism? This isn't a selfish question. It's an important question to which a cogent answer must satisfy you and inspire you to take action. Therefore, I ask you this question with great interest. Naturally, only you can answer the question.

PERSONAL EXPRESSION AND A MORE FULFILLING SOURCE OF HAPPINESS

Like the terms *manager* or *management*, *happiness* is overused and often reduced to Hallmark card pleasantries. We all want it, and we have difficulty pinpointing what it means. Yet happiness is part of the optimistic climate. Rather than taking you through a philosophical discussion about happiness, let me boil it down simply.

There is happiness that generates pleasure, which is fleeting. Then there is happiness derived from meaning, self-awareness, and growth in life that helps a person become fully functioning: pursuit of one's best self. Research shows that the latter type of happiness is more satisfying and has longer-term effects on our psychological well-being.[3]

Researcher Alan S. Waterman invited 140 undergraduate and 69 graduate students from Trenton State College, New Jersey to participate in his happiness study in the early 1990s. Each student was asked to complete a Personally Expressive Activities Questionnaire, which began, "If you wanted another person to know about who you are and what you are like as a person, what five activities of importance to you would you describe?" Then the students were asked questions measuring the two concepts of happiness mentioned previously—happiness that generates pleasure and pursuit of one's best self.[4]

Notice that the question Waterman asks focuses on identity and meaning. He's not asking students what makes them feel good. Here we can begin to uncover the ingredients necessary to know how you'll benefit from creating a positive work climate. It starts with discovering what in your work brings you meaning. Do you tap into curiosity to understand your beliefs and behaviors that could help you become a better human being, a better leader? How frequently do you seek out opportunities to help you grow professionally?

In all of Waterman's research hypotheses, he forecast that the happiness that would help an individual become his or her best self would be shown to be more advantageous to the pursuit of excellence.

As part of Waterman's research, he found that personal expressiveness was integral to and more strongly associated with the activities the students identified in response to his question. Personal expressiveness is a combination of factors: sense of identity, self-actualization, internal locus of control, and doing what's best for the greater good.[5]

The presence of these four factors can positively influence the development of your potential and that of your employees. This is key to answering what benefit you'll get from creating optimism. In short, the benefit to positively shaping the climate for your team is getting to know yourself better and discovering how to fulfill your own potential. You position yourself to love your work. In doing so, you set the tone and lead the way to help your employees realize their own potential and find greater meaning in their work and in life.

Leadership axioms that advocate caring for people first miss one important step: You must first care for yourself. To genuinely create a climate of optimism and advocate its business value, you need to tend to your own happiness triggers and discover meaning and purpose from your work. If you can't do that for yourself, your efforts to help others will be limited.

Happiness Reflection Question #1
What one or two activities in your personal life fulfill you? For example, activities that "make time fly."

Happiness Reflection Question #2
What one or two activities in your professional life fulfill you?

Happiness Reflection Question #3
What immediate next step can you take to integrate more of the personally and professionally fulfilling activities into your week? Your month?

Another important element to loving your work, and thus helping you positively influence your team's work climate, is an integrated life. Stewards today diligently integrate their personal and professional lives. It's not about finding balance—balance is bunk. These two worlds will always compete for your attention. It's a zero-sum game: One part of your life will lose, and that's hardly the outcome I want for you.

Stewart Friedman, author and professor at Wharton School at the University of Pennsylvania, explains in *Leading the Life You Want* that we need to learn skills for being real, whole, and innovative. According to Friedman, being real is about knowing what's important to you. Additionally, being whole means understanding how the different aspects of your life affect one another. Finally, being innovative is acting creatively to accomplish what's important. These skills, according to Friedman, are key to integrating all the roles you play in your life.[6] We lose ourselves and our identity when we cannot successfully integrate—and switch gears in—the roles we play: employee, leader, husband, wife, son, grandparent, friend.

Self-Actualization, Internal Locus of Control, and Helping People

In psychologist Abraham Maslow's hierarchy of needs, self-actualization is at the peak of the pyramid. We know today that Maslow's belief that we move up the pyramid when each level is satisfied is outdated. We can go up or down the pyramid without fully satisfying each level. You can work on self-actualization even if your safety needs, which are at the pyramid's base, are not fully met.

The key is that you continuously work to grow your potential. Waterman explained that personal expressiveness is experienced when "activities are ones through which individuals advance their highest potentials, that is, their potential excellences."[7]

Undoubtedly you will experience setbacks personally and with your team in your work as a steward. What's key is how you overcome and respond to issues. More important than that, however, is that you are building a solid foundation of a healthy self-identity and a strong focus on helping others. A steward with an internal locus of control believes she creates her own success and controls the direction of her life. Not one of us achieves our highest potential while blaming people and circumstances for setbacks.

The final factor in personal expressiveness taps into our human nature. We are wired to desire contributing to something bigger than ourselves. Actively participating in work that links purpose, meaning, and passion to advance the greater good is deeply satisfying.

It's not the pursuit of happiness that matters. What matters are the actions we take that bring happiness beyond the fleeting experience of pleasure. What you stand to gain from cultivating optimism is not only a better climate or more engaged and productive employees but greater awareness of yourself and your leadership presence. Not only does this bring forth a gratifying sense of accomplishment, but you are helping others live up to their full potential.

CONTAGIOUS POSITIVE EMOTIONS

It may not take much to imagine being in a room with other managers positioning and arguing for employee pay increases. Such meetings can be highly contentious, fueled by a range of emotions. For this reason, the annual conversation managers have about pay increases made for an ideal research setting to help researchers at Yale University learn how emotional contagion influences group performance. (Emotional contagion is when a person's positive or negative emotions are sensed and mimicked by other people.) In the study done at Yale, 94 business school undergraduates had two minutes to make a pitch for why their employee deserved a pay increase. The participants had two goals: Get as large a pay increase as possible for their employee and maximize the use of funds to the greatest benefit of the organization. If in the allotted time the managers did not reach consensus on the proposed raises, no one would receive one. Each management group consisted of two to four people, including an actor to spice things up a bit during the discussions.

Yale University professor Sigal Barsade found that teams with high levels of positive emotions performed best: They cooperated with one another and experienced less conflict. Sigal concluded that "people are 'walking mood inductors,'" influencing moods and behaviors.[8]

What's intriguing about Barsade's research is not just his conclusions. It's that we intuitively know that our moods, our emotions, influence group interactions, yet many of us don't alter our moods to help a group perform better. Our emotions are contagious and influence how people feel. How people feel influences the quality of their work. The emotions people experience shape their willingness to connect and deepen relationships. It's a powerful insight for leaders to leverage when working to shift to the optimistic workplace.

The best-known psychologist and professor of positive contagious emotions is Barbara Fredrickson. She has made it her life's work to understand how positive emotions influence others. Her research reveals that when we witness positive acts, it inspires those who see them to extend the gesture to others. Her research reveals that positive emotions broaden our "ideas about possible actions, opening our awareness to a wider range of thoughts and actions than is typical."[9] In other words, we broaden our capacity to act positively based on the good actions of another person. The positive emotions we experience then help us build new skills, connections, and knowledge, and have a positive impact on other people.

Consider Catherine Ryan Hyde's novel *Pay It Forward*. The main protagonist, Trevor McKinney, has a school assignment to do something that has the potential to change the world. The basis for Trevor's project is for people to spread positive, contagious emotions by doing something nice for another person. There's one requirement in the project: If someone does something nice for you, you have to pay forward a kind deed for a stranger and expect nothing in return. Trevor's project sets off a chain reaction that touches the lives of many strangers and ultimately attracts media attention.[10]

I'm not intimating that you set into motion a national buzz of contagious emotions. I am suggesting, however, that you pause long enough to understand the influence positive emotions can have on you and those on your team. Own the emotions that you're spreading. Or said more straightforwardly, your mood affects the climate and the emotions your employees experience at work.

Fredrickson developed the broaden-and-build model from her research findings. The foundation of the model is the belief that positive emotions help people perform at their best levels and have a lasting impact on their growth and development. Outcomes, according to Fredrickson's research, include increased creativity, self-awareness, resiliency, and a better, socially adjusted person.[11]

The benefit to the organization is through mimicry of the positive emotions. As the steward of your team, expressing such positive emotions as joy, gratitude, serenity, interest, hope, pride, amusement, inspiration, awe, and, yes, love can positively influence how others feel and experience work.[12] But how does the expression of positive emotions work?

Mark Fernandes recounted for me the day he punched holes in the drywall in the corporate office. He left after his wall-punching episode and figured he no longer had his job. The former bouncer from South Philadelphia with a 26-inch neck let his rage dictate his emotions. Unexpectedly, the CEO from the office with the smashed-up walls called and wanted to see him the next day. "You can't be tearing up my shit," Charlie Luck said, as he opened the conversation with his slight Southern drawl. He arranged for Fernandes to stay with the company, and that was the beginning of a nearly 30-year friendship in one of America's top aggregate businesses—Luck Companies.

Luck is headquartered just outside of Richmond, Virginia. Employees would tell you they make little rocks out of big ones. Founded in 1923 by Charles Luck Jr., Luck Companies is in the aggregate business. The big rocks it crushes are used on highways and other infrastructure projects. The stones it mines are used to decorate homes and even build tennis courts. Luck has over 800 employees in its four business units. One of those units, Luck Stones, is a major regional player among national competitors, the 16th largest in its industry.

The heart of Luck Companies is blue-collar work, supported by white-collar professionals. All new employees must spend time in the quarries where rock is mined. It takes a deep appreciation for one's roots to keep a solid focus on the portion of the business that pays the bills. It would be easy for marketing or finance to be absorbed by their work realities and forget about the hard physical labor that goes into keeping the bills paid. When I talked with employees in the corporate office, the reverence and connection to their heritage was obvious in their personal stories about the time they spent in the quarries when they started at the company.

The connection to the organization's history starts at the top with CEO Charlie Luck. Luck's commitment to honor a long company tradition of focusing on the relationship with employees and their families is refreshing. His passion for people is contagious.

Case in point: Charlie saw beyond Mark Fernandes's anger: He saw Mark's potential. Or, as the company's mission proclaims, he saw human potential that needed igniting. Charlie's positive emotions of interest and hope are contagious. Today Mark calls himself a "recovering jerk." The extension of positivity from Charlie had a transformative impact on

Mark. It was enough to eventually help him understand a different way of approaching people and living his life. Growth and awareness have helped Mark transform how he leads, inspires, and relates to people.

Charlie could have expressed anger toward Mark. He could have fired Mark. Instead, Charlie's contagious positive emotions demonstrated his belief in Mark. Can we not use more of this approach in our workplaces? Far too often we allow our frustrations with work and people to spread negative emotions, creating tension and adding drama to our work relationships. It's a slog to do great work in a negative work environment. Optimism will struggle to emerge or thrive. Without contagious positive emotions, we miss the opportunity to change lives. We miss the opportunity to help people find value in themselves and purpose in their work. We miss the opportunity to catapult results to higher levels that help the organization's effectiveness.

The broaden-and-build model puts in place the opportunities for your growth and your team's. It contributes to a climate that gives people hope and the belief in doing work that enriches their lives and provides meaning. Through your stewardship, you can create or enhance this type of climate for your team.

Barbara Fredrickson says positive emotions emerge from how we make sense of events and ideas. Lonnie Bissonnette is a living example of this. Bissonnette is a paraplegic BASE (Bridge, Antenna, Span, Earth) jumper. He jumps from bridges with a parachute attached to his wheelchair. His life in a wheelchair is the result of a horrific accident doing what he loves: extreme sports. Because a parachute accidentally wrapped around his leg as he was jumping from a bridge over Canada's Snake River, Bissonnette hit the water headfirst, crushing his neck, spine, spleen, a lung, and many other body parts. Despite spending five months in the hospital and advice to not BASE jump again, Bissonnette was undeterred. He believed he could continue to jump, and he turned that belief into reality by retooling a wheelchair that was suitable for bridge jumping.

Looking at this event through the lens of positivity, emotions of joy and pride are immediately obvious. I can only speculate on the emotions Bissonnette experienced. With both a growth mindset and positivity, Bissonnette did not let his circumstances hold him back from pursuing what was important to him. Simply put, he viewed his paralysis as merely another factor to consider when planning a jump. Bissonnette's positivity is contagious. Friends, strangers, and TV and online media outlets were inspired by his belief and actions. They helped Bissonnette evolve his passion to fit his current circumstances.[13]

Similarly, choosing workplace optimism is a leadership act that requires you to assess your own circumstances—good or not—and act to improve them even if no one asked you to. The tragic news for most workplaces is that employees don't believe in their bosses' intentions. In a study released in 2013, Ohio-based consulting firm Root found that employees are skeptical about their leaders' intentions and inability to develop relationships that motivate and inspire performance. According to the study:

* 22 percent of employees believe management has employees' best interest in mind.

* 68 percent of workers think managers are more focused on their own growth than on inspiring others to be successful.

* 38 percent agree that their boss has established an effective working relationship with them.

* 26 percent agree that managers in their company embody the values desired in employees.[14]

A steward pivots and addresses these tragic numbers through, for example, gratitude, interest, hope, pride, and inspiration. Such stewardship would be innovative. It would be provocative. And it's necessary to achieve sustainable business results. Your people aren't expecting anything to be done to counteract Root's findings. The moment you begin to do something about the dismal climate strangling your team's performance is the moment your people begin to pay attention again.

Reflection Question #1
What is the mood of your team's work environment?

Reflection Question #2
Using the list of positive emotions from Barbara Fredrickson, how might you intentionally use one or two to inject more optimism into the climate?

Implications of Positive Emotions

So how do you assess your own work environment? The implications of positive emotions can guide us through this question. It's important to note that you cannot instill emotions in people.[15] How others respond to you is a matter of choice and awareness. What's key is to examine your acts of leadership and be mindful of how they might appear to others and how your actions might evoke positive or negative emotions. Another benefit to having positive emotions is how they help you discover meaning in the work you do. While a conscious effort is necessary to purposefully shape the climate, it starts by setting an example. That's why creating workplace optimism starts with you—the person immediately responsible for the well-being of the team and its members.

Table 3-2 on the next page shows the implications of positive emotions. With them are questions to help you assess your circumstances and find meaning in your work. The goal of these questions is to help you uncover what you can proactively do to tap into the benefits of positivity. A summary question to ask yourself is, "What next steps do I take?"

You are the steward of the work climate. You get to help your people achieve their greatest potential through their work. At the same time, you have your own needs and potential to tend to. As a steward, you can care for what isn't yours by demonstrating what that care looks like by taking the steps to find fulfillment and meaning in your own work. This is the highest-order personal benefit: Model what you want for and expect from your team, and grow from the effort. Creating an optimistic climate takes diligent personal work. It reinforces personal significance and team performance.

Table 3-2. Positive emotions implications.

Positive Emotions Implications	Insight and Actions
Inspire people to overcome challenges	What challenges might your team need to overcome?
	What are the benefits—personally and for the team?
	What actions might you take to positively help the team move forward?
	List the reasons why you want to help move the team past challenges that compete against the goal of enabling optimism to emerge.
	Who might help you with your goal?
Set a positive leadership presence	Identify one to three people of whom you can ask the following question: "What is your experience of me as a leader?"
	Make notes of what works and what doesn't.
	Commit to continue doing the things that work by recruiting an accountability partner.
Increase fulfillment from your work	Identify what work is meaningful that you currently do and would like to do.
	What makes the work meaningful? Who makes the work meaningful?
	What are you most proud of in your work?
	How can you help your team members find meaning in their work?
Strengthen relationship with your team	Where can you create more connection between you and your team?
	What are the growth areas for each of your team members?
	What is each of your team members' strengths, and how are you maximizing them?
	Where can you increase the degree to which your team feels "in" on decisions?

CHAPTER 4

The Downside of Optimism: Missteps and Excess

*If you fall prey to the temptation to constantly search for
something positive to grab on to in hopes of eliminating,
hiding, or concealing negative emotions,
you will lose in the game of life.*

—TODD KASHDAN AND ROBERT BISWAS-DIENER,

THE UPSIDE OF YOUR DARK SIDE

Optimistic work environments are energizing. Yet you need to be mindful about ignoring the nonoptimistic realities influencing your team. To do so will create a false sense that everything is okay. The truth is, work can be damn right infuriating. Even though the positive climate helps employees do better work and creates joy, your team is not impervious to the downsides of work life. So it is important to know the potential missteps and excesses that can surface when cultivating optimism in the climate.

THE COMMON MISSTEPS

In my work with clients, few initially believed in the influence climate could have on a team's performance, morale, engagement, and overall life satisfaction. It's no surprise, then, that the first misstep is to not believe optimism in the workplace is even possible. Certainly doubt about the possibility is natural. So, too, is doubting that you can pull it off. To have some skepticism is okay. In fact, it's healthy. Yet it's crucial that you have some belief that optimism could emerge from your intentional acts of stewardship. With a healthy dose of skepticism to evoke your curiosity, and the belief in the possibility of optimism to inspire you to actually do something, you can make a strong first step to correct the missteps.

Misstep 1: Believing It's Somebody Else's Responsibility

In the hundreds of conversations I've had with others about workplace optimism, invariably the point is made that it must start at the top. As I mentioned in Chapter 3, this is a fallacy. This belief lets us off the hook from doing something about the bad vibe hovering over teams. A CEO's support alone would not make the difference anyway. For a climate of optimism to be possible, it is best initiated at, and supported by, the middle layer of the organizational hierarchy, assuming there is one.

The immediate leader has the greatest chance at causing change and achieving the desired results. With this in mind, believing or waiting for someone else to take responsibility for the climate is a common misstep that can be remedied. How? Grab a piece of paper to answer the following questions:

* What would you gain by creating a climate of optimism?

* What would your employees gain? The organization? Your customers?

* What would it feel like if optimism was present in your team's climate?

✳ What would happen if you didn't do anything to create the conditions for optimism?

✳ What's the first step you would need to take to shift the climate to be more optimistic?

✳ Which one or two people could you build an alliance with to support your taking action?

Ultimately it's your belief in the value of this work that will help you avoid the misstep of believing it's somebody else's responsibility to create an optimistic workplace. It's natural to question the validity of the work. Keep your eye on why you're doing this whenever you come across obstacles or when you doubt yourself. You will run across barriers. You will doubt yourself. That's okay. You're building something meaningful that can help you and your team find great fulfillment in work.

Misstep 2: Failing to Build Alliances to Support Your Effort

The last question above had you think about whom you could develop an alliance with. This is key. You want to have a support structure in place to encourage you to keep up your great work. Here are a few essential things to consider when identifying allies:

✳ You can have honest conversations with them.

✳ They are comfortable challenging your thinking.

✳ They believe in action and are not all talk.

✳ They genuinely believe the Origins of Optimism—purpose, meaningful work, and extraordinary people—are important elements for an organization to be successful.

Your allies don't need experience with creating an optimistic workplace. You only need to trust and respect them. You might want to consider choosing someone who is in your peer group and someone younger than you. Diverse perspectives are invaluable to help bring about change. Your allies' viewpoints will help you grow, and their input will strengthen your plan.

Misstep 3: Assuming You Know How Your Team Members Feel About the Climate

While it may be tempting to draw conclusions about what your team members think of the climate, don't do it. You're likely to be overly critical or downplay reality. Either one will lead you astray. You risk over- or under-engineering your plan to shift the climate. In my experience working with clients, the best place to start is to have conversations with your team.

No matter the size of your team, select a diverse group of team members. Choose a few who you anticipate would be supporters of creating workplace optimism. Then select a few who may be skeptical. Select one person who you anticipate would find fault in the idea. Be careful here, however. Too often leaders will spend more time with those who resist new ideas, believing if they can convince the nonbelievers they have a chance. This is another fallacy. By spending more time with the resisters, you risk alienating those who would support you and the would-be supporters.

Schedule one-on-ones with those you want to talk to. Keep the conversation simple and focused on what's possible. Here are a few questions to consider:

* What three words would you use to describe what it feels like to work on our team?

* How would you personally benefit if the work environment was more optimistic?

* What immediate actions would you recommend I take to improve the work environment?

Of those three, the first should be the lead question. Follow it up with one of the other two to dive a little deeper into each team member's perspective. Be mindful to not get defensive; it will stop short a productive conversation.

Your goal is to encourage a dialogue. Ask open-ended questions, avoiding *Why* questions (for example, "Why do you feel that way?" or "Why does that matter?"). Those questions sound confrontational or place doubt in your team member's mind. It's natural to want to know more. Instead of asking why, be sure you sound curious, not accusatory: "What's important for me to understand about your perspective?"

Misstep 4: Assuming People Understand the Importance of Their Work

Thought leader and author Patrick Lencioni says people need to hear the same message seven times before finally getting what you're saying.[1] Too often, however, leaders think because they said something important once, people will remember it. Certainly this trap has snared many stewards when it came to the topic of work alignment.

Work alignment occurs when each person on your team knows how her contributions align with the team's and organization's goals. While this is a standard leadership belief, it's not often put in practice.

At the core of helping employees see how their contributions fit into the bigger picture, you need to leverage purpose. Specifically, help employees understand their purpose in the organization: why their roles exist and why they matter to the team's and organization's success; how their strengths and talents influence outcomes and other people. Connect each team member's projects to key strategic initiatives or team goals.

It's common for people to fall into rote patterns of work, leaving their hearts and minds at home, so creating a climate that's optimistic requires a lot from you and from your team. As adults, we need to understand why something matters or is a necessity. Merely requesting, or worse, barking your needs may get compliance. But compliant people are not loyal. They don't apply their talents to be creative or innovative in a manner that's effective. Compliant employees are less adept at change; they've learned to rely on being told what to think and do.

When employees understand the importance of their work, they take ownership of their results. Additionally, when you set clear goals and explain why the work matters to the team or to the organization, you enable progress.

Researchers have discovered that progress in one's work is key to engagement and is driven, in part, by clarity in purpose and direction.[2] Employees invest discretionary effort to do their best work. They are more willing to try different approaches when older ways of doing things don't yield desired results. In short, when you treat your people as mature, fully functioning adults, you will have an easier time helping them see how they fit into the organization's plans.

As a steward, your goal is to help your team develop a broad understanding of their work and the personal meaning inherent in it. To drive the point home, research from the Hay Group found that managers in high-performing companies spent 30 percent of their time "understanding others' needs, and coaching and developing team members."[3] This is how you successfully show your people the importance of their work.

Misstep 5: Unknowingly Overpromoting Individualism

No employee works alone at Menlo Innovations. Every week employees are paired with a new colleague. The pairs work on assigned projects; then each employee takes on a new partner the following week. This approach differs vastly from what happens in most organizations.

Physically separated from one another by cube walls, offices, and/or geography, most workspaces promote individualism and not team cohesiveness. Even goals are set for individual performance. Rarely are team goals established and monitored. Not only is team cohesion compromised but so is a shared mood, both of which are vital to a positive work climate.

The benefits Menlo Innovations gets from its pair-partners tactic are many, chief among them group solidarity. Team members learn to lean on one another to deliver results; each week the work is handed off to a new pair of partners, who must be prepared to answer client questions or address their needs. Without solidarity and strong emphasis on clear communications, Menlo's client commitments would often fall short.

Pair partners may not be realistic for your team, but the benefits of cohesion are central to your endeavors to shift the vibe of your team. How, though, do you shift an embedded focus on individuals to a collective mindset without jeopardizing the feeling of autonomy? This is where emotional energy becomes important.

Randall Collins, a University of Pennsylvania sociologist, explains that emotional energy is the outcome from people who enjoy interacting with one another. Their enthusiasm from working and spending time together drives them to want to interact. Collins calls this interaction ritual chain theory. While there is a physical element to it—the importance of physically getting together—a cognitive element is also important.[4]

Our memories of how enjoyable the interactions are create a desire to repeat them. When emotional energy is shared among a group of people, a strong bond forms, and the desire to repeat the interactions is high.[5] Think of a great vacation you took with family or friends. The time you spent together often leads to a conversation about wanting to do it again. Shared stories strengthen the relationships. Mementos from the vacation serve as symbols of the trip, another way to unite people and create a shared experience.

Similarly, the key to creating optimistic workplaces is to shape the conditions and plan for the opportunities that create emotional energy. Collins says it's important for your team to get together physically, at meetings or conferences, for example.[6] You should protect the team from outside influences that could undo the positive climate you're creating. Ensure that the team has a shared focus and mood. Your goal is to build bonds between team members. A team bond helps shield people from any toxicity that might come from outside the group.

You also need to ensure that internal toxicity doesn't poison the climate and prevent emotional energy. Overpromoting the rugged individual inevitably positions your people against one another. This tears at the team bond that's important to a healthy climate.

Reflection Question
In what ways might your actions promote the rugged individual? What are the impacts to people? To the climate?

To avoid the misstep of overpromoting individualism and undermining your plan to create workplace optimism, here are some areas for powerful action that can help you strengthen group cohesion:

❏ *Team Goals.* Have the team identify goals that encourage collaborative behaviors, for example, a targeted percentage of team projects delivered on time, improved customer satisfaction with team performance, even higher satisfaction with internal, two-way communications. Make the measurement of goals part of the group process. Measure the goals annually or semiannually. Ensure the results are shared with the team and coupled with conversations about how to improve the results.

❏ *Group Planning.* Methods such as Agile project management rely on a team to plan work in sprints. Sprints are often 20 to 30 days long but can vary. Hold monthly meetings with your team to plan what can be done for the month given the team's project workload. Hold the team accountable to decide what commitments it can make. At the end of the sprint, review commitments and repeat the process. While Agile may be mostly associated with technology projects, I have successfully used it for organizational change management projects. Agile practices help slice ambiguous, big projects into smaller chunks by focusing on work that is most important at the moment.

❏ *Broad-View Coaching.* This is spending time helping each team member connect his work to his actions, to the team's and the project's success. It's an intentional conversation that reinforces autonomous thinking and commitment to the team's success. These coaching conversations should occur quarterly at minimum. I recommend holding them monthly for new employees or for employees adjusting to a focus on group solidarity.

❏ *Celebrations.* Successful teams execute, but they also celebrate. Celebrating accomplishments helps create and sustain emotional energy. More simply, it helps boost morale. I see too many teams and organizations that have a lopsided perspective in which the focus is solely on executing plans and achieving goals. From a human performance perspective, a myopic view on results can lead to burnout, fatigue, and distress. The irony is this adversely impacts a person's and a team's ability to execute with precision and stay in a high-performance zone.

Randall Collins's research points to some strong indicators that emotional energy is helpful to create memorable interactions, or what he dubs "collective effervescence." You'll begin to see team members supporting each other more vigorously in accomplishing their goals. Individuals show their enthusiasm for the work and for what the team is accomplishing together. Imagine this as a rush of emotional energy. Its infectiousness influences team bonding behaviors. One such outcome is that team members begin to adopt symbols that represent their relationships.[7]

Finally, you'll notice that there is a shared sense of what is right and wrong influencing behaviors, decisions, and interactions.[8] These are powerful outcomes that you want to monitor for their impact on workplace optimism. Your role is to encourage team members' behaviors that support these outcomes and have conversations individually and as a team when behaviors don't support the team's success. No one person is more important than the team. This is your motto as you endeavor to create optimism.

> *No one person is more important than the team.*

TOO MUCH OF A GOOD THING?

Pat Christen had been thinking about the role harmony plays in the workplace. As the CEO of HopeLab, Christen wondered aloud with me the role it plays in work life. She and her senior management team were exploring ways to lean in and effectively navigate the tension between caring about people, having difficult conversations when a team member's performance is off, and staying true to the nonprofit's purpose and associated work. Maintaining harmony requires diligence and a perceptive leader or leadership team that notices how the climate influences employees' beliefs about the workplace.

The question of harmony in the workplace doesn't often surface as a healthy inquiry unless the climate is maturing. This is precisely the place Christen and her leadership team found themselves.

Though they helped create an optimistic work vibe, the leadership team wondered if harmony would be possible if people avoided difficult conversations or productive conflict. Could the optimistic climate at HopeLab be too much? More broadly, is it possible for an optimistic climate to have deleterious effects? The short answer is, yes.

What are the signs and outcomes of an excess of optimism? Let's look at them and at what you can do to lead your team away from too much of a good thing.

Sign of Excess #1:
The Struggle from the Balance of Opposites

HopeLab wrestles with the struggle from the balance of opposites—the natural and necessary tension between harmony and discord. Harmony exists with the successful coming together of the three elements of workplace optimism: purpose, meaningful work, and extraordinary people.

When those three elements come together, a single, continuous narrative emerges, explaining their effectiveness: Purpose reveals meaningful work that inspires a community of extraordinary people to contribute and advance the purpose of the team. Optimism becomes too much of a good thing when it leads to a false sense of harmony.

Discord doesn't eradicate harmony, however. An optimistic work environment can withstand it, keeping harmony in check. Let's look at an example where the tension between the two was not effectively navigated.

I had been working with Larry (not his real name), who wanted to promote more of his team's accomplishments and downplay anything that might upset or discourage people. The belief was that if Larry and his team had a big enough megaphone shouting good news, the team members would feel better during the difficult times they were experiencing. Unfortunately, this belief is a common ailment of old-school management: Employees rely on information from managers to understand what's happening in the business.

Without the struggle from the balance of opposites, employees become cynical. When only good news is shared and leaders don't acknowledge the influence discord has on the climate, employees' well-tuned BS detectors signal "fraud." Stewards understand that employees see and hear when things are not working. They talk with customers. They work with broken processes and begrudgingly adhere to 20th-century policies that make no sense in today's workplaces. If all they hear is rah-rah chatter from leadership and watered-down acknowledgments of problems, trust in the stewards is weakened, and optimism suffers. Confidence is shaken.

How HopeLab gracefully balances the tensions inherent between harmony and discord is in the importance it places on relationships. It's assumed people have the skills to handle difficult conversations or conflict.

Over lunch with HopeLab's vice president of culture and leadership, Chris Marcell-Murchison, I discussed how the organization handles the tension between harmony and discord. First, team members attend workshops that provide them with tools that deepen their self-awareness. This is key for all of us. When we help employees become more self-aware, we are helping them be more productive in life and contribute at a higher level in life—personally and professionally.

Second, there is an intentional effort to lead through the impacts of discord on teams. HopeLab's philosophy is to talk about where disharmony is present and resolve it. The difference between HopeLab's approach and Larry's is the belief that discord is necessary.

The need for BS detectors is abandoned as a survival mechanism to make sense of the work environment. Instead, healthy discourse and relationships flourish because the tension between harmony and discord is accepted as necessary.

Greater levels of trust are possible because the truth is not swept under the rug and replaced with a false sense of security. While discord is uncomfortable, its presence combined with harmony helps create an honest understanding of the messy realities inherent in our relationships.

Reflection Question
How can you balance the tension between harmony and discord to help your team achieve greater results?

Sign of Excess #2:
The Country Club Effect

Country clubs are exclusive for a select group of people. They have a fun, carefree environment and offer a wide range of activities. Members are spoiled with five-star service. The country club provides an experience that is not widely available anywhere else. These clubs are an escape from the realities of life.

In the context of the workplace, when a team becomes isolated from the realities of business, the country club effect emerges. Keeping people "happy" becomes more important than holding them accountable for commitments and results. People become accustomed to being special.

An excess of optimism can lead a team to feel so good about its environment that it loses sight of business realities important to the organization's success. For example, in one organization I studied that typically is marked by optimism, a team was so focused on helping people achieve their fullest potential it lost sight of its performance goals. The leader shortsightedly focused on personal achievement, overlooking holding people accountable. By all appearances, the team was aligned with the company's beliefs. The team's leader didn't see that there were performance problems. She was blinded by optimism. But a closer look at the team's financial performance revealed that a lack of accountability was minimizing the team's capabilities. Sure, the leader cared for her people, but she was failing to have important performance-based conversations—good or bad.

Caring without accountability is the primary driver of the country club effect. In some cases the goodwill and good feelings from optimism become so comforting that leaders stop holding people accountable for results. They don't want to jeopardize the positive influence the work vibe has on people.

At the heart of this problem is a leadership breakdown. In a conversation, Mark Fernandes, chief leadership officer of Luck Companies, told me he believes leadership breaks down when a leader doesn't hold people accountable to a commitment; it causes confusion. For example, if I ask you to do something by a certain date and let you get by without delivering by the due date, what's right and acceptable is muddied.

Unfortunately, the country club effect means that there is a feel-good environment where little progress is made on important work. Employees don't clearly understand how they're performing. An imbalance emerges with an overemphasis on relationships needed to foster community and an underemphasis on work and results needed to advance the team's and organization's purpose. Purpose becomes diluted. Work's meaning is a distant consideration. Employees view work only as pleasant and comfortable.

The country club effect is like fleeting happiness: It feels good in the moment but can quickly dissipate when something bad happens. The country club effect results from pursuit of pleasure: Does working here make me feel good? A leader's preference is to avoid or downplay matters that might disrupt feeling good.

While it may be tempting to settle for the country club effect, stewards purposefully navigate their teams away from such an alluring, shiny object. How? Shift your stewardship to focus on the psychological well-being elements from Carol Ryff's work highlighted in Chapter 2:

❑ *Unleash employees' potential by finding opportunities that deepen their skills.* Hold them accountable for following through on their commitments. Make the same commitment for yourself for this to be effective.

❑ *Build a relationship with each person on your team.* Get to know the whole person, not just who he is and what he does at work. Spend time in your one-on-ones learning about each employee's passions in and outside of work. Learn what she believes her purpose is in life and at work. And if she doesn't know, encourage her to discover it. We'll explore this more in Chapter 6. But for now, reflect on the business value of having employees engaged with life and how this could positively influence their performance on the team.

❑ *Increase employees' self-awareness.* Help them find meaning in their work. Coach them to understand how they influence others, positively and negatively.

An optimistic work environment is one that brings out the best in people. Value is placed on relationships that respect the whole person, not just the employee. Research shows that work is currently an area in life that brings little richness to employees' lives.[9] Where the country club effect can crumble is by helping work become a positive influence in areas that research shows are key to bringing deep levels of happiness and meaning: family, health, relationships, and personal growth.

Be mindful, however, of the dignity and respect trap inherent with the country club effect. Treating people with dignity and treating them with respect are justified behaviors in overcaring environments.

The problem with dignity and respect is they're not enough. They need to be paired with a commitment to help people achieve their goals or, as Mark Fernandes told me, "become the best version of themselves." Dignity and

> *The problem with dignity and respect is they're not enough.*

respect may make people feel good, but the feelings evaporate when there is little else to accompany them in the workplace.

Sign of Excess #3: Overreliance on Advocates

Optimism bias occurs when you interpret an event in a way that benefits you, ignoring other realities or truths that may refute what you want to see or believe. In this case, a steward's optimism bias favors advocates over pragmatists.

Advocates for workplace optimism are important. However, advocates can fall into the trap of blindly promoting its importance, ignoring contrarian perspectives. The favoring of only advocates shapes team members' perceptions and signals that contrarian viewpoints are not welcome. In other words, don't upset the climate by speaking ill of it.

Remember, the immediate leader has the greatest influence on how employees perceive and experience the climate. Therefore, your behaviors have significant influence on how your team members make sense of the work experience.

The preference for advocates sends an unintended message that going along with the program is expected. The overly rosy climate can silence pragmatic employees—those who may need more information or evidence of progress before supporting the importance of workplace optimism.

Reflection Question
Who in your group of confidants can you rely on to hear the unfiltered truth about your team's work environment?

Just as optimism bias can cause you to overlook what you don't want to see, cognitive dissonance can prevent you from taking the actions to counter the bias. Cognitive dissonance occurs when you encounter new information that conflicts with what you believe, value, or hold true. For example, let's say you realize that the advocates are overly rosy in their outlook of the team's climate. You know you should listen to other perspectives to get a balanced understanding about how the climate makes people feel, but that might conflict with your own rosy estimates, so you don't. And if you do get a more pragmatic take, you might not accept it for the same reason.

This sign is more difficult to overcome than the previous two. It requires that you be open to hearing information that you might not want to hear. Additionally, someone from your team or a trusted peer needs to feel comfortable talking with you about a preference for advocates. The reality is that both advocates and pragmatists are important.

The solution for this sign is in building and nurturing authentic relationships with peers and team members, relationships where confidants can freely share their thoughts, even if unpopular or difficult to hear. The consequence of this is that someone will likely feel more comfortable pointing out the bias in your perspective.

Another solution is asking for feedback. When you take on the work to shift the climate, you need feedback and input on what is and is not working. Asking for feedback not only develops trust, it deepens it, too. It gives you credibility. If ever there was a secret weapon to steward development, it's seeking feedback—positive and constructive.

Sign of Excess #4: Inflexible Methods

Research from Hay Group lists flexibility as a key dimension of climate that positively shapes employee perception and performance.[10] The consulting and research giant explains flexibility as the absence of rules, policies, and procedures that make no sense and only interfere with people doing their best work.[11] It's Netflix abandoning its expense report policy and procedure and trusting people to act in the best interest of the organization. But let's look at the opposite: inflexibility.

Inflexibility is a result of too much comfort with the way things are. It's change inertia; there's little willingness to adapt to the shifts triggered by exterior and interior business influences. Management innovation expert and theorist Gary Hamel explains organizational inertia this way: "[Organizations] are frequently caught out by the future and seldom change in the absence of a crisis. Deep change, when it happens, is belated and convulsive."[12]

You are the steward of the work climate. You get to help your people achieve their goals and aspirations. Too much control and inflexible rules and policies hamper people's performance and, consequently, diminish optimism in the workplace. It's a natural human desire to want to control one's circumstances, even at work. Hampered performance leads to people feeling frustrated. Bloated methods—policies and procedures—go unchanged despite their growing irrelevance.

> *Status quo breeds mediocrity, calcifies bureaucracy, cripples progress, and hampers changeability.*

When an optimistic climate goes unchecked, it's possible to be reassured by its benefits and overlook changing what no longer fits in the workplace. Eyes that were once watchful grow sleepy. Arrogance creeps in and challenges arguments for changing what has led to success: "Why fix what isn't broken?" This viewpoint breeds mediocrity, calcifies bureaucracy, cripples progress, and hampers changeability. Ultimately it negates the positivity inherent in climates marked with optimism. In short, inflexible methods signal that leaders have become too comfortable. The policies and procedures necessary to run the business become outdated. The benefits of workplace optimism become threats when inflexible work practices fail to adapt.

Further evidence that this excess example is undermining a positive workplace can be found in what employees talk about. If employees regularly express frustration with archaic rules or policies, it's time to look into revising or eliminating them. At some point, the complaining stops when no action is taken or no evidence of change is on the horizon. The vocal dissatisfaction goes underground, which is not good.

The rules and policies in question here are those that hamper your team's ability to do great work. When employees can't do their best work, the optimism in the climate is diminished. Let's say your company doesn't allow employees to work remotely. Despite the growth in technology to help remote workers be productive and the trend that employees want this flexibility, your organization fails to revise its policy. Not only does this make it difficult to attract top talent because so many organizations offer this, it frustrates existing employees. It becomes a distraction that unnecessarily interferes with the cultivation of workplace optimism.

Table 4-1. Potentially outdated rules and policies.

Potentially Outdated Rules and Policies	Steward Actions to Eliminate Inflexibility
• Remote work policy • BYOD policy • Physical work environment layout • Side projects • Performance reviews policy • Coaching and mentoring policy • Team, individual status • Volunteer program • Customer experience • Bonus policy	• Review approval for remote working requests. • Revisit who gets a work-assigned mobile device. • Update design approach of physical work environment. • Review how side projects are approved. • Review recognition programs and practices in your team. • Review goal-setting philosophy and practices. • Refresh one-on-ones format. • Update how you assign work based on employees' strengths. • Update how you set employee development goals and opportunities. • Expand your multichannel communications. • Implement stand-up meetings. • Broaden and update your decision-making philosophy. • Implement skip-level meetings: employees meet with their boss's boss.

Reflection Question

What policies or rules can you revise to help add more flexibility into the workplace?

You should identify the inflexible methods that might interfere with your work to create an optimistic workplace and see if you can influence changing the rules and policies that cause them. Table 4-1 on the previous page includes common rules and policies that you should consider evaluating.

CHAPTER 5

Values-Based Leadership

Leadership today is an inside-out job in that it's more about
who the leader is versus what [he] knows.
—MARK FERNANDES, LUCK COMPANIES

A SHIFT IN PERSPECTIVE AND EXPECTATIONS

She looked at me with stern eyes, arms crossed, and said, "We are not here to help people self-actualize." My mouth went dry, my heart rate quickened, and my anger flared. I had been asked to put together a recommendation to increase the participation rate of the employee tuition-reimbursement program where I worked. A core tenet of my proposed overhauled program was to increase employees' overall life satisfaction. This included paying for classes that didn't have anything to do with an employee's immediate job. If someone wanted to take classical guitar lessons because it's something she always wanted to do and brought her some happiness, then the organization could benefit from the goodwill and commitment to the employee. At least that's how I framed the recommendation.

The chief human resources officer had smacked down my idea without considering the purpose of the recommendation. And she was not open to hearing the logic behind my thinking. I knew in that moment that I could no longer work for her. She had trashed several personal values of mine—service and learning—and I no longer could work to support her vision. Soon thereafter, I left to start my own organizational change consulting practice.

I'm not alone in how I'm guided by my personal values and how they help me make sense of my work and find meaning in it. According to a 2013 study from Net Impact, a nonprofit organization with a mission to drive transformational change in the workplace and the world, 58 percent of students who participated in the study would take a 15 percent pay cut to work for an organization with values like their own, and 74 percent want to work for an organization that shares their values.[1]

The same research shows that 80 percent of students want work that makes the world a better place. This includes working for an organization with a philosophy of practicing corporate social responsibility and having an impact on society and the environment. In contrast, 39 percent of students say it is important to work for a prestigious employer. What's intriguing about this research is the importance placed on lasting, meaningful work elements. Contrast the high percentages related to the importance of values and meaning against prestige. Values and meaning win hands down. With students representing the future of work, there is a message of change for all managers: Shift your mindset and actions to reflect the changing tide in worker attitudes and expectations or risk being irrelevant.

We all have personal values. Most of us live by them intuitively. If you were asked what your values are, you'd probably recite some ubiquitous ones that may or may not be part of your core identity.

Personal values require reflection on your life events to know them deeply. Values require purposeful action to integrate them into how you live and lead. To know your values is to have insight into why you make decisions, with whom you make friends, or the type of work you pursue, or don't. It's been said, "If you don't stand for something, you'll fall for anything." Knowing your personal values helps you know where your line in the sand is— what you'll tolerate and what you won't.

> *Knowing your personal values helps you know where your line in the sand is— what you'll tolerate and what you won't.*

Research categorizes personal values into two groups: terminal and instrumental. Terminal values reflect the outcomes of your actions. In the example that opened this chapter, my desire to help employees improve their overall life satisfaction was the goal. The terminal values of service, meaning, and purpose underlay my intention.

Behaviors feed into the second type of values, instrumental. Instrumental values are the modes of behaviors, or the means to achieve the goal.[2] For example, my value of creativity and risk taking helped me reimagine the tuition reimbursement program to be more inclusive of what would be considered eligible for the program.

For me, the assignment to overhaul the tuition reimbursement program strongly aligned with my values. So the response from the chief human resources officer cut deep for me. Her inability to inquire into my thinking was offensive. The situation was exacerbated by her unwillingness to look into her own biases.

I would be remiss if I didn't acknowledge the chief human resources officer's values set and its influence on her interaction with me. Admittedly, I can't say what her values were. In hindsight, I could have sought to understand where she was coming from before shutting down. However, I share this example to illustrate the powerful influence values have on our lives, whether we're aware of them or not. At the time of this example, I hadn't done the personal work to identify, know, and show my values. Intuitively, I knew that the interaction was a deal breaker for me.

KNOW AND SHOW YOUR VALUES

"How deeply do I care about our common future? How do I actually make a positive difference?" These are questions leaders are asked to answer at Luck Companies.[3] These questions are not rhetorical—they are central to the aggregate company's values-based leadership philosophy.

Employees are expected to know the answers to the above questions and are provided the tools and learning opportunities to look within themselves and honestly answer them. Mark Fernandes, chief leadership officer, says, "The single biggest [influence] on how leaders show up day in and day out" is when leaders know their personal values. He goes on to explain that the company believes making money is a result of helping employees create meaning in their work and in their personal lives.[4] Luck's leadership model must be working—it contributes to a 91 percent associate engagement score as measured by Hay Group. Compare this to the global average engagement score of 28 percent.[5]

So, what lessons can we glean from the strong work Fernandes and Luck are doing? For starters, creating a strong, positive work climate relies on leaders who know their personal values, align their actions with the company's mission, and develop a love affair with employees. A great place for you to start is to identify your values so you can know and show them in your day-to-day stewardship of your team.

> *Making money is a result of helping employees create meaning in their work and in their personal lives.*
> —MARK FERNANDES

At the heart of Luck's values-based leadership model is what the company calls "Leader Being" and "Leader Doing."[6]

Leader Being focuses on who the leader is as a human being. While some organizations ignore this aspect of leadership and pass it off as "soft," Luck takes on this deeply personal investigation; the organization supports leaders' introspective exploration through 360-degree assessments and values and personality assessments.

A leader's introspective exploration into their being is then made into hard performance measures that apply to frontline leaders through to the C-suite. Luck has created a VBL Index that indicates how well leaders are leading and is used to help make compensation and succession decisions.[7]

Two-thirds of a leader's pay is determined by values-based leadership. One-third is based on a yearly, 360-degree assessment, looking to see if the leader is walking the talk. The second third is based on the leader's team engagement results. The engagement survey measures how the leader is impacting work and the company's associates. The company's CEO considers the day engagement results are posted to be the "most important day" for the organization. Think of it as a report on the state of the organization. Finally, the last third of the index is based on business results—sales and cash-flow margins, for example.

Luck's Leader Doing portion of its philosophy focuses on the demands of the job. It's tied to the final third of the VBL Index. Fernandes says Luck is constantly evaluating "how we balance the quest for profits and what's right for our people." What's important about Fernandes's insight is that values-based leadership must ultimately generate value for the organization. Where Luck stands apart from most organizations is in its belief that it must also generate value for its people.

Identifying, knowing, and showing your values help prepare you to be a more effective, compassionate, and understanding steward. In short, you are more relatable because of a deeper, evolving awareness of what you stand for, which attracts and appeals to others. To identify, know, and show your values helps guide your decision-making process. Harvard Business School professor and former CEO of Medtronics Bill George explains in his book *True North* that doing these things helps you find your direction as a leader. Knowing your values helps guide your interactions with your employees, family, and friends.

Unlike in my interaction with the chief human resources officer, where I hadn't identified my personal values, you can draw upon your values to shape conversations and influence your behaviors by modeling a more encouraging way to show up as a leader—your Leader Being.

Another important benefit of being a values-based steward is increased consistency. When others can rely on your mostly predictable ways of being, their confidence and trust in you increases. Erratic or unpredictable behaviors cause concern, diminish trust, and weaken chances of others seeking you out for guidance. This scenario is useless to a steward.

When it comes to creating a positive work environment, employee well-being is a central driver. Knowing your values is critical. They promote the exploration of your true self and help you live in accordance with that person. Expanding on this idea, when you live in accordance with your true self and exert effort to do good, virtuous work, you experience being fully alive, fulfilled, and doing what you're meant to do. This is what researcher Alan Waterman calls personal expressiveness. Your values paired with your well-being and personal expressive-

> *Unpredictable behaviors cause concern, diminish trust, and weaken chances of others seeking you out for guidance.*

ness are the gateways to creating a rewarding experience as a steward.[8]

Values work begins with identifying values. Table 5-1 is a table of values. Select the top five that resonate most with you. For an interactive experience in identifying your values, you can visit Luck Companies' Values-Based Leaders blog. There you can download a free app to guide you through selecting your values. Visit http://igniter.valuesbasedleader.com/dashboard to download the values-identification process. You can also download all the exercises included here from the book's website: www.theoptimisticworkplace.com.

Table 5-1. Personal values.

Accountability	Accuracy	Achievement	Aesthetics	Appreciation
Challenge	Collaboration	Community	Competence	Creativity
Curiosity	Decisiveness	Effectiveness	Excellence	Fairness
Freedom	Fun	Generosity	Growth	Hard Work
Harmony	Health	Integrity	Joy	Justice
Learning	Loyalty	Privacy	Prosperity	Relationships
Resourcefulness	Responsibility	Results	Serenity	Stability

Loyalty Is Not Dead

Loyalty isn't dead. People need a reason to be loyal. We don't readily give loyalty to others. It needs to be earned through a trusting exchange of opportunities for results. Too often, old-school managers hide behind their titles and assume loyalty is given to them. Stewards don't assume it's automatically given because of positional authority. It has always been something given after proving one's worth it. It's about trust. It's about results on a human level. It's based on efforts and intention. Loyalty is given when we honor our word and promises.

You build loyalty through knowing and showing your values. Loyalty is key to an optimistic work environment. It's what keeps people from leaving when times are tough or a better opportunity presents itself. More importantly, however, loyalty helps create and deepen relationships. People are less likely to leave an organization when they invest time to get to know others and to be known. In today's talent wars, you can't afford to lose good people. Use your values to be your genuine self and ultimately build loyalty by attracting people who want to work with you.

> *Loyalty isn't dead. People need a reason to be loyal.*

Give people a reason to share that which they reserve only for those trusted enough to earn it.

Define Your Values

Now that you've identified your values, it's important to know what they mean to you. While it's essential work for you as a steward to unleash each of your team members' potential, it's also important to explore what unleashes *your* potential. Knowing yourself is a vital pursuit for anyone interested in shaping the climate to be marked by optimism. So take the time to define carefully for yourself your top five values in Table 5-2 below. If you don't like to mark up your book, go to the book's website to download the worksheet. Here are a few things to consider when developing definitions for each value:

1. Use your life's events to define each value. Looking up the definition of the word is a shortcut and only limits your connection to the value.

2. Use words that resonate with your experiences. Imagine explaining the value to other people. Would they associate the value with you?

Table 5-2. Your personal values defined.

Value	Definition
_____	_____
_____	_____
_____	_____
_____	_____
_____	_____

Show Your Values

The event had come to an end. Danielle Aaronson, a Luck Companies employee, was helping with the cleanup while her boyfriend, Zach, who was visiting Luck, was hanging back waiting for her to finish up. Charlie Luck, the CEO of Luck Companies, had stayed after the event and introduced himself to Zach. Much to Zach's surprise, Charlie spent 30 minutes chatting with him. Aware of how much time Charlie had spent with him, Zach offered a reason for Charlie to excuse himself. "You're obviously important to one of my people. This matters more than any email, anything that I have to take care of," explained Charlie. For Danielle, it was a special moment. She told me, "It felt really beautiful to be considered that important to someone who technically is that important."[9]

Charlie values relationships. He takes time to show their importance through his interactions with others. Setting the tone for what's important, Charlie's emphasis on relationships ripples out across the organization. While that is a great example of stewardship, it isn't the primary point. The point is that Charlie's behavior aligns with the value of relationships. Danielle and Zach felt special because Charlie made time to show how important they were to him.

Now it's time for you to think of ways to bring your values to life. In Table 5-3, list behaviors or ideas that bring to life your values. Use the example to help you with this critical step.

Table 5-3. **Personal value behaviors.**

Value	Behaviors
Relationships	• Block time on my calendar for one-on-ones with each employee to learn what or who is important in my employees' lives. • Each quarter take my team to coffee to discuss success and lessons. • Identify 2 to 3 industry events I want to attend to expand my professional network.

GETTING EMPLOYEES TO
THINK THE SAME WAY

Each morning, the mechanics at Luck Companies gather in a circle to discuss the day's work. But before that conversation begins, they first tell stories about demonstrating values in their work. It's a morning ritual. Now imagine this support for values-based leadership among your employees.

What would it take to begin integrating values-based conversations within your team? It would begin by modeling the way, sharing your personal values with your team. Tell the team why it's important to you to know your personal values. Open up by explaining what insights you got from doing the values exercises in this chapter:

* Encourage your employees to complete the values exercises in this chapter by downloading the worksheets from the book's website.

* Hold a team meeting to discuss insights.

* Ask your team members how knowing and living by their personal values could be helpful to them in their work.

* In your one-on-ones with employees, explore more personal ways they can live and work by their values. Help employees identify where their values aren't present in work and where they are. Build a plan to strengthen the alignment.

SHAPING A MORE PERFECT FUTURE
FOR THE WORLD OF WORK

A more perfect future is a workplace that reinforces employees' knowing what they stand for by way of their values. Furthermore, such a work environment, through your stewardship, encourages employees to know themselves and to continue the lifelong pursuit of unraveling what's important to them and who they are. An optimistic work climate is shaped by the steward's belief that a person is not a position or a function: A person is a human being who has a story and life goals. Bob Chapman, CEO of Barry-Wehmiller, said to me, "Leadership is about people, purpose, and performance. It starts with the fundamental responsibility to [the] people whose lives are entrusted to us" and inspiring them to live a life full of purpose.[10] This changes the very nature of work. It is no longer about a "What have you done for me lately?" mentality. Rather, it's about how you help people become better human beings. You do this so they have a richer life and also contribute their best when at work.

When I interviewed Chapman, he told me a moving story that reinforces the importance of the intersection of personal values with a more human workplace. A project team had presented its successes to Chapman and other executives. The project team had successfully improved work quality and reduced lead times—important business outcomes. Yet Chapman wanted more. So he posed a question to the employee representing the team: "How did it affect your life?" The employee replied:

"Do you know what it's like to work in a place where you come in every day? You punch in on a time clock; you go to your workstation. Management tells you what to do; nobody ever asks you what you think? You get 10 things right, and you never hear a word. You get one thing wrong, and you get your [butt] chewed out. [The organization] complains about your salary; they complain about [paying] you benefits, but they don't give you the tools you need to do a good job. I realize now with our [current] leadership that I used to go home feeling not so good about myself. I'm a different person when I go home now because I'm contributing to making things better; people are asking me what I think. I'm working together with my team to make things better. And when I'm nicer to my wife, she talks to me."[11]

At Barry-Wehmiller, the stewards place significant focus on understanding the relationship between work and a team member's personal life. This focus is a result of Chapman's value of family. With his awareness of this value, Chapman's stewardship is driven by doing his part so that people have both rich professional and personal lives. He creates a climate of optimism by zeroing in on the influence work has on his people's personal lives.

The employee responsible for the project realized that he is a different person because he can connect his work to a bigger purpose. Chapman learned from the team lead's story that the way people are treated at work affects their personal lives. The two worlds are "dramatically interconnected. The way we lead affects the way others lead," Chapman told me.[12]

Consider the implications of Chapman's insight about the influence leadership has on others. As a steward, this is an insight to take to heart. As a steward, who is responsible for people and things you don't own, taking responsibility for the influence and impact your relationship has or doesn't have is important to creating a positive workplace. The outcome of knowing and showing your values is a greater awareness of who you are. The awareness significantly influences how you show up as a leader. Consequently, you begin to create the stickiness that holds your team members together and helps them begin to see a positive picture of the workplace and of their team. Connecting the dots further, this helps shape the climate and supports your effort to create workplace optimism.

A SENSE OF IDENTITY

"A sense of identity is not so much something to do, as it is someone to be," observes psychologist Alan Waterman.[13] Merely knowing your values does not mean you have a clear sense of identity. It's not the act of naming your values that makes the difference. It's how you express them in your life and in your stewardship that matters. When your values are incorporated into your being they facilitate a deeper understanding of who you are as a leader. Furthermore, the pursuit to discover and uncover your identity as a steward helps you uncover your potential. This pursuit becomes something you model for your team members, setting the example for them to discover and uncover who they are and how they can live up to their potential.

> *It's how you express your values in your life and in your stewardship that matters.*

Charlie Luck doesn't view his role as CEO as the top dog running the show. It's quite the contrary. He told me, "Our most powerful work is the impact on people." Such an outcome is born from associates understanding themselves and others. The pursuit to understand and to be your true self leads to a sense of feeling right in actions, a sense of centeredness in life, clarity and strength in purpose, living into your purpose, competence, and fulfillment from work and life.[14]

If this all sounds like it doesn't belong at work, keep in mind the financial successes of both Luck Companies and Barry-Wehmiller. Both organizations encourage and, quite frankly, expect their team members to be mature, fully functioning adults evidencing personal inquiry of who they are and how they show up as leaders.

Luck Companies believes that employees must first work on themselves to make a difference in their work and on coworkers. In fact, Luck hones in on five behaviors that focus on deepening a person's sense of identity so he can positively impact others. The following list is from the company's *Values Based Leadership Journal*, which is given to all new employees:

* Be aware: Know who you are, where you are, and what's going on around you.

* Align: Draw strength from your core values.

* Understand: Learn what others think, feel, believe, and need.

* Adapt: Modify your behavior for the situation and the person.

* Act: Do the right thing for the right reason at the right time.

Values give direction to your life. Know and incorporate your values into your self-awareness. This will help guide your pursuit of meaningful personal and professional goals. To have an evolving sense of identity is energizing and infectious.

The expression of your personal values cannot be withheld while working. Work is a major part of your identity. If work is not a positive experience because of a lack of autonomy, purpose, passion, and meaning, you will likely feel dissatisfied in your overall life. It's not possible to divorce your personal life from your professional one. The two worlds need to fit together in a manner that stimulates the pursuit of your highest potential as a human being. This starts with knowing and showing your personal values.

From increased confidence to deep, personal happiness, the pursuit to amplify your understanding of your sense of identity is fundamental to shaping your positive work experience and that of your employees. At a time when only 55 percent of employees say their leader inspires them, the heavy lifting needed to deepen your sense of identity is not only needed but can bring you a sense of accomplishment and belonging within your team, even your organization.[15] The late, great business thinker Peter Drucker famously posited a simple yet profound question we all must reflect on and ultimately answer: "What kind of person do I want to see in the mirror in the morning?"[16]

CHAPTER 6

It All Starts with Purpose

For those who don't embed purpose into their companies,
at best these companies will underperform and at worst,
they will perish.
—JOHN LEBOUTILLIER, PRESIDENT OF UNILEVER CANADA

The first element of the Origins of Optimism is purpose. Purpose is the reason you do something. It might be a calling. It might be a matter of ethics. Purpose calls each of us to act in a way that may be unpopular or different from what most would say, do, think, or feel. Deeply personal purpose can and should be shared. It is the ultimate guide to your way of living. In the business world, it guides your stewardship.

While it may be easier to categorize purpose as a construct important to spirituality or religion, science is discovering the importance purpose has to our well-being. In this chapter, I'll reference recent scientific studies that bring us surprising insights about the role purpose plays in living a fulfilling life and its relationship to business. In the context of creating workplace optimism, purpose acts as an inspirer and an anchor. It inspires you to lead and coach people to a higher level of performance. It anchors you in times when it may be convenient to go down a path simply because it's quicker and easier.

Purpose sits on your shoulder and whispers in your ear what the ethical thing is to do. A strong steward listens and acts according to purpose.

IKIGAI—REALIZING THE VALUE
OF BEING ALIVE

Your health is linked to a sense of purpose in life, or, as the Japanese call it, *ikigai*. *Ikigai* is defined as "joy and a sense of well-being from being alive" and "realizing the value of being alive."[1] A 2008 study in Japan by Toshimasa Sone and his colleagues sought to understand how, if at all, *ikigai* contributed to longevity in life. Sone and colleagues studied over 49,000 Japanese adults over seven years to learn the association between *ikigai* and mortality.

What the researchers found was encouraging for those who had clarity in purpose. Mortality risks were higher in those who did not have a sense of being and of joy. Those lacking clarity in intentional living had a higher incidence of cardiovascular disease and other life-threatening illnesses. Ninety-five percent of Japanese adult research participants with *ikigai* lived seven years longer than the 83 percent of the study's participants without a sense of meaning and purpose in their lives.

While it can't be said scientifically that understanding the value of intentional living automatically leads to longevity in life, the study presents a strong case for the value of knowing your purpose and the potential positive impacts to your well-being. Purpose can inform the choices you make and the behaviors you intentionally demonstrate as a leader. These can ultimately be parlayed into a healthier life.

Psychologist and researcher Carol Ryff includes purpose in life as one of the six elements of well-being. She defines purpose in life as "the tendency to derive meaning from life's experiences and possess a sense of intentionality and goal directedness that guides behaviors." Ryff finds that purpose helps us recover from negative events, potentially helping to slow down the effects of aging.[2] Both the *ikigai* study and Ryff's work concluded that improved living can be linked to a purpose-centered life. Ryff came to her conclusions about the role purpose plays in life differently than did the Japanese study. She studied people's eyeblink reflex.

Purpose and Your Eyeblink Reflex

Imagine participating in a research study where you are shown different types of images at varying times. You're shown images that are a mixture of positive, negative, or neutral themes to measure your emotional response to what you see. Ryff and her colleagues designed this study to test how quickly people emotionally rebound from seeing negative images, clinically known as startle probes, compared to positive images, or recovery probes, and neutral images.

Researchers use startle probes to measure the reflexive eyeblink caused by the stimulus, in this case an image. This method of measuring eyeblinks is known as eyeblink startle reflex, which is also a way to help measure people's emotional states. It's done by measuring the length of eyeblinks.

Measuring the length of eyeblinks gives researchers insights into the participants' emotional responses to pictures. The longer the eyeblink the more unpleasant the response. Ryff's research focused on determining if having purpose in life helped people recover faster from negative emotional stimuli.

The study raises some interesting questions: If having purpose helps a person recover from difficult situations, would it help the person to be strong in the face of difficulties? How could perceived negative situations benefit a person? Why is purpose important?

What Ryff and her fellow researchers found was that those with purpose in life, positive relationships, and demonstrated self-acceptance had a quicker recovery time after viewing a startle probe. The quicker recovery time suggests that the person could adapt his response to the stimulus faster and in a more healthful way.[3] Researchers Todd Kashdan and Patrick McKnight suggest that purpose is foundational to a person's identity.[4] Purpose serves as an anchor and helps a person be more resilient in the face of difficulty, or seeing images that evoke an emotional response.

Purpose gives clarity to what is important and guides us through the day-to-day barrage of input from the external world: the temptation to find shortcuts in work, a decision to confront a colleague over his behavior, setting aside time to spend with a loved one. Imagine how purpose can guide you in your personal and professional endeavors. It can help you recover from negative situations faster and get on with dealing with reality, avoiding feeling bad or sorry for yourself.[5]

> *Purpose serves as an anchor and helps a person be more resilient in the face of difficulty.*

The eyeblink-rate study also showed that we can improve our future health and quality of living simply by knowing what makes us thrive. Fundamentally, it helps you build a solid foundation from which you can pursue your personal and professional aspirations intentionally.

In short, knowing what your purpose is helps you deal with whatever is thrown your way and inspires you to take actions in alignment with it.

So what does this mean to you, a steward intent on shaping the conditions of workplace optimism? Certainly the implications are likely to be personal and rooted in your circumstances and life experiences. There are, however, positive outcomes when you uncover your purpose or more strongly align with it. You may:

✳ Bounce forward when recovering from negative situations.

✳ Increase your ability to be motivated to learn from negative situations.

✳ Have greater fulfillment in your work and in your personal life.

✳ Experience more rewarding integration of your work and personal roles, transcending work-life balance.

✳ See an increase in your capacity to remain clearheaded during stressful, demanding times.

✳ Increase your willingness to help others find and align with their own purpose.

✳ Experience lasting enjoyment of your work through an increase in your intrinsic motivation.

✳ Let go and recover quicker from the emotional hangover of negative situations.

✳ Have greater awareness of and control over your emotional response to demanding work and life situations.[6]

That list makes it clear that purpose is more than a spiritual pursuit to learn how to fulfill your destiny. While spirituality or religion can play a part in your journey to know why you are alive, it's not the only requirement.

Exploring your own potential and incorporating a purposeful mindset into your stewardship approach can be a difference maker for you and those whom you lead. Having clarity in your purpose influences how you guide your team to achieve results. The depth and quality of relationships you create are richer and more meaningful. And as previously discussed, your well-being can also be positively influenced.

PURPOSE, BUSINESS, AND YOU

Personal purpose has been segregated from the business world for too long. It's an unnatural bifurcation of your two worlds. Clarifying your purpose is essential to your leadership. It's no longer enough to focus on *what* you do as a leader. It's *how* and *why* that rounds out your effectiveness and your ability to work alongside people. Executives are realizing that clarity in purpose is key to "accelerating their growth and deepening their impact, in both their professional and personal lives," said Nick Craig and Scott Snook in a 2014 *Harvard Business Review* article.

Craig and Snook completed research that found that less than 20 percent of leaders know their personal purpose.[7] Leaders without a clear purpose risk struggling with health issues and show a lack of consistency in their leadership style. Business, its customers, and certainly employees are better positioned for providing or experiencing fulfilling work when led by stewards who passionately pursue their own purpose with relentless vigor and curiosity. It sets the gold standard for stewardship.

> *Personal purpose has been segregated from the business world for too long.*

Purpose goes beyond creating shareholder value. It's about more than personal financial gains. With that in mind, Unilever CEO Paul Polman explained in an interview in *Rotman Management* that any company's business model must benefit society. Going a step further, Polman explained that this should ultimately benefit a company's shareholders, but the pursuit of purpose should not be driven by them. Businesses themselves rather than shareholders must take the responsibility to be a purposeful business.[8]

Just as it's a business choice to do business purposefully, it's also a personal choice. It's antiquated to believe that the pursuit of purpose and its revelatory nature is reserved only for executives. The business benefits when all people know that their purpose can be experienced on a grander scale and are encouraged to pursue it. The risks are minimal and payoffs are considerably more rewarding.

DEFINE YOUR PURPOSE

Todd Kashdan and Peter McKnight explain that there are three dimensions of purpose: scope, strength, and awareness.

According to Kashdan and McKnight, the scope of your purpose refers to how common it is in your life. The researchers explain that the centrality of purpose shapes the thoughts and emotions that impact your actions.

Strength of purpose is the intensity with which purpose shapes your thoughts, emotions, and actions. If your purpose is to help people live up to their potential and its strength is powerful, you'd believe in finding ways to maximize a person's strengths and likely feel good about doing so.

The final dimension of purpose is awareness. That's simply a matter of how self-aware you are and whether you can articulate your purpose. Kashdan and McKnight explain that the greater your awareness, the stronger your ability to adapt your behavior to different situations.[9]

So, how much consideration have you given to your purpose? Knowing your purpose comes from constant reflection and exploration of your life. Purpose is not static; it's dynamic. It evolves along with your unfolding understanding of your roles in life.

As a steward interested in creating or deepening optimism at work, your awareness of purpose positions you to be more grounded in who you are. In turn, you are more emotionally available to your team members. This helps your employees feel more appreciated, needed, and accountable. The following questions are applicable to everyone. It doesn't matter if you know your purpose and are fully leveraging it or if you are thinking about it intentionally for the first time. The questions are designed to help deepen your awareness of the role that purpose has in your life. They will also help bring to light the type of impact you want to have on people and/or the world.[10] Find a quiet place to reflect on your answers to these questions:

✳   Write down the meaningful or rewarding behaviors from your work. Challenge yourself to look beyond experiences that immediately draw out your attention. What might be "hidden" from your immediate observation?

✳   From the meaningful or rewarding behaviors, what new insights do you notice about yourself? What meaningful or rewarding behaviors are confirmed?

✳   How do you know if the behaviors are lasting elements of who you are?

✳   When in your life were you most energized? Think of as many possible examples as you can. What were you doing? For whom were you doing the energizing activity? What value did you get from the activity?

✳   What themes do you notice underlying your responses? What insights do the themes hold?

✳   What obstacles in life positively shaped your way of living? Consider examples even if at the time you didn't think it was positive.

✳   What values of yours do you see in your examples? Are any values missing? What insights does the values alignment provide?

✳   Now consider who was involved in your examples. What role did each person play? What support did they provide? Did someone not provide support? What does this indicate to you? Who would you go back to and thank for their role? Why?

✳   What did you learn about yourself from the examples you referenced?

✳   Has an event in your life caused you to reevaluate what's important to you? If so, what changed for you? How does the event influence your purpose, if at all?

✳   What makes your heart sing? Are you doing enough of that in your life? How could you increase doing more of what makes your heart sing? Does it spill over into your work or personal life?

✳ When you observe others, what behaviors yield results that
   you like? (For example, people who volunteer could make you
   feel good about having a positive impact on others.)

You'll likely come back to these questions repeatedly. Some may be
difficult to answer. As I mentioned previously, living in alignment with
your purpose requires constant reflection. It's normal to spend time
reflecting on your answers. In fact, reflecting on your purpose is something you never stop doing.

I strongly encourage you to seek input from those who know you
best. We have blind spots preventing us from seeing aspects of our
behavior, personality, and identity. Input from others will help deepen
your insights and round out your answers. After you get input from others, go through the questions again. Make any changes you think are
appropriate.

On a personal note, I revisit how my work aligns with my purpose
throughout the year. I define, redefine, and review my goals as the year
progresses. I use the end of the year as a time to plan what I call big
rocks—big goals that stretch me outside what's comfortable. Jim Collins calls these "big hairy audacious goals." It works best for me to set
these types of goals annually. I create a colorful physical presentation
that documents my purpose and goals. I carry it everywhere with me. I
review it often to ensure I'm focusing on what matters most. When I'm
not doing work that matters, I explore what needs to shift, what I need
to stop doing. This can take time to change. As long as I'm taking action
to have what matters most to me and my purpose, I feel there is meaning in my life.

WHEN PERSONAL AND ORGANIZATIONAL PURPOSE COME TOGETHER

"Business is here to serve society," Paul Polman said in a 2014 interview
with McKinsey & Company. Polman explained the unifying role purpose
plays at his company.[11] From advocating that women love themselves in
Dove's "Campaign for Real Women" or Ben & Jerry's social conscience,
purpose is central to Unilever's business philosophy.[12]

In the 2014 interview, Polman said businesses have a responsibility to actively improve the realities that give them life. It's a modern take on the role of business in society. To play an effective part, businesses must act like social servants, and they require leaders with purpose. But teams and businesses need to be clear about their purpose, too. When personal and organizational purposes come together, a powerful force is unleashed. It transforms aimless work into calls to action.[13]

It's feasible to work for an organization with a purpose that doesn't fully align with your own. If you've only begun to think about your purpose, what you'll likely experience is a calling to be in an environment that satisfies you more deeply. This doesn't mean you can't have such a desired environment where you are now. For many, transforming the current workplace can be richly purposeful. For a steward, creating workplace optimism is a purpose-driven activity. What makes the endeavor so gratifying is the positive influence it has on your life and the lives of others. This is what makes climate so powerful.

Workplace optimism helps people feel that where they work is a positive part of their lives. For example, Alice Cabrera-Bryant, a financial analyst at HopeLab, told me that the organization's climate and culture motivate her to go to work. "It's part of the connection that I'm going to have with people here in the workplace," she explained to me. Her connections with coworkers inspire her "to do something just for the good of it and because it makes me feel good."[14]

In cases where personal and organizational purpose come together, the benefits discussed at the beginning of this chapter are magnified. Organizationally, benefits, some of which are measurable (such as increased engagement; employee well-being; improved sense of identity; and increased productivity, innovation, curiosity, goal clarity, and accountability) can catapult the organization to higher levels of performance.[15]

PURPOSE AND RESILIENCE

One final factor is worth noting when it comes to personal purpose: the importance of resilience and its influence on purpose. When resilience is combined with *ikigai* and Carol Ryff's eyeblink-rate research is taken into account, the role of purpose begins to show its transformative influences on how we relate to our work and to others. *Ikigai* points to joy in living; our overall psychological well-being positively influences how we deal with difficult situations or people. Resilience shows our capacity for working through and overcoming and growing from the difficulties that are part of living.

There are strong undercurrents of resilience in Ryff's eyeblink-rate research. Interestingly, HopeLab found through its own research that resilience could be strengthened when a person has a sense of purpose. When creating workplace optimism, all three inputs—*ikigai*, improved living, and resilience—position purpose and people to flourish. The overall quality of your life can improve. This can shift how you relate to people. This is where the magic occurs in your stewardship: You can better relate to people because of a greater awareness of who you are. In turn, you are better positioned to help people develop.

Lynda Gratton, professor of management practice at the London School of Business, highlights the importance of inner resilience in a work context. Without inner resilience, she believes, employees won't have the energy to live up to their full potential.[16] This adversely affects organizational performance. Not only can an unoptimistic work environment diminish employees' ability to achieve performance goals, but it also weakens resiliency-building behaviors.

> *Resilience can be strengthened when a person has a sense of purpose.*

We respond more positively to our environment when we grow as human beings. And this is how you can begin to shift or deepen optimism in the workplace. Stewards accept the hardships that come with guiding a group of people to fulfill their individual potentials. They take the hits and push through the tough times with their actions anchored in purpose. Stewards celebrate the victories, small or large. Resilience is what makes stewards fighters, and the best ones are both tough and compassionate.

I learned about the importance and relationship of resilience to optimism when spending time with team members at HopeLab. HopeLab's purpose is to improve human psychological and physical well-being through the use of technology.

The winner of the prestigious Drucker Award for Nonprofit Innovation in 2014, HopeLab has proven why it's a destination workplace near Silicon Valley. With a workplace climate that leaves employees feeling joyful, fulfilled, and "seen"—CEO Pat Christen's words for acknowl-edged and respected—HopeLab has been able to develop award-winning technologies that make a difference in people's lives. What a powerful way to unite people for a common cause. Furthermore, what a magnet for attracting people who want purposeful work.

The organization's strong sense of purpose has no room for people who just want to collect a paycheck. A strong, compelling purpose attracts purposeful people. HopeLab's games Re-Mission 1 and 2 were invented to help young cancer patients improve their health through an app that encourages them to complete their cancer treatments. The games accomplish this by showing young patients how the treatments fight cancer. A usual outcome for game players is a belief that they can beat the disease.[17]

The nonprofit is now turning its attention to using social technolo-gies to promote resilience. It will be fascinating to see how HopeLab can inspire developers, designers, scientists, and philanthropists to use mobile apps with the purpose of making life better. In the meantime, HopeLab is learning how to integrate its lessons in resilience to strengthen its workforce. As it so happens, it is influencing its climate to be more positive—to be optimistic. HopeLab defines resilience as three psychological characteristics: sense of purpose, connection with people, and control or agency over one's actions.[18]

A Lesson in Purpose from HopeLab

A sense of purpose is created through an environment of belonging and promoting "empathic concern in the world."[19] The latter is evidenced through HopeLab's purpose as expressed through its inventions such as Re-Mission. The influence on workplace optimism can be profound. Getting to help people live healthier lives or giving cancer patients hope has a positive influence on employees' perceptions of their workplace. The positivity is contagious.

Employees are encouraged to create an environment that helps col-leagues feel like they belong. Whether it includes making snacks for peers or choreographing a flash mob to celebrate a coworker's last day, a welcoming, positive work environment paves the way to optimism.[20]

It's our innate human desire to belong, to feel connected, and to have a sense of purpose. Such basic desires need to be leveraged if you are to transform the work environment to be positive. HopeLab works diligently to create an optimistic climate through cultural elements like inclusion, holding people accountable, and having high performance expectations. These three elements help staff experience positive emotions, shaping how they feel about work and the workplace.

It would be a stretch to say all employees at HopeLab feel a sense of purpose working there, though those I spoke with had a clear sense of purpose. Here are some ways it was demonstrated in my interviews. See if you notice any of these signs in your team:

* Employees take ownership of work results to the point of questioning the intention of the work's value.

* People actively pursue personal growth opportunities.

* Emphasis is placed on supportive, collaborative working relationships.

* Contagious, positive emotions bring out the best in team members.

* Large discussions and smaller conversations center on how one's work supports a bigger picture.

* You can see the value and understanding when work is handed off from one area to another.

* People are aware of how one's actions impact others.

A sense of purpose calls on us to behave in ways that stretch us outside our comfort zones. As Nick Craig and Scott Snook astutely observed in their *Harvard Business Review* article, your purpose doesn't come from your education, life experiences, or the skills you've picked up along the way. Rather, your purpose is rooted in your identity.[21] To know this you need to be willing to reflect on your life and not reject such a notion as some new age idea that has no room in business.

The consulting firm Deloitte found in a 2013 study that executives (68 percent) and employees (66 percent) agree that most businesses don't create a sense of purpose or do enough to deliver impact that's meaningful. The study stresses that purpose can create a competitive advantage through employee development programs, service, and products that have an impact on clients and that benefit society.[22]

Robert Wong, vice president of Google Creative Lab, says purpose is the most important element for unifying a team. Wong says the era when the manager was central to success has ended. Purpose is now central to retaining employees, who presently have more choices to pursue purposeful work. With purpose, Wong says, you can keep talent from leaving. The aspirational becomes practical.[23]

Reflection Question #1
How might you initiate conversations about purpose with your employees?

Reflection Question #2
How will you and your employees benefit if you help them incorporate purpose into their reasons for working with you?

Aligning Purposes

HopeLab has a clear sense of purpose, and the organization's employees are, on the whole, deeply aligned with it personally and professionally. How deeply does your purpose align with your organization's? The following questions are designed to help you connect your purpose to those of your organization and your team. Like the questions asked earlier to help you identify your purpose, this is an iterative process. Your circumstances change, as do your perspectives about work and your role as a steward.

* What is your organization's purpose?

* What is your team's purpose? How does your team support the ultimate purpose? Where is there alignment between the organization's purpose and your team's? Where can you tighten the alignment?

* What is your purpose? What evidence is there to show alignment between your purpose and your organization's? What

about alignment between your purpose and your team's?
What's missing?

＊ What immediate next steps can you take to make alignment stronger?

＊ What immediate next steps can you take to address purpose misalignment?

＊ Who are allies who can help you better align your purpose with those of the organization and your team?

＊ What themes do you notice in your answers? What is the significance? Does the significance change your immediate next steps?

In a 2014 study by The Jensen Group, 69 percent of workers said they believed they could achieve their dreams through their own efforts. Twenty-nine percent said they could achieve their dreams in their current work.[24] In a different study, 72 percent of employees indicated that work that affected causes important to them was essential to their life goals.[25]

More people than ever are pursuing freelance work, and it's projected that by 2020 more than half of the workforce will be free agents. Organizations need leaders who can create the conditions important to attract talent. In fact, 91 percent of students responding to one study named work environment and culture as one of the most important job attributes.[26]

While it's important for you to have an evolving sense of your purpose, it's equally important for you to support your staff's exploration of and learning to live with purpose. Optimistic climates support employees' exploration of purpose. The support for purpose awareness is not solely an act of stewardship; it's an acknowledgment of humanity. And we can use more humanity in our workplaces.

CHAPTER 7

The Meaning Makers

Today, business leaders cannot begin to foster a climate of positive order if their sole concern is making a profit. They must also have a vision that gives life meaning, that offers people hope for their own future and those of their children.

—MIHALY CSIKSZENTMIHALYI, *GOOD BUSINESS*

A BRIGHT SPOT

Of all the domains in your life—work, family, health, personal growth, social relationships, spirituality/religion—work occupies most of your daily wakeful hours.[1] While family and social relationships are mostly associated with meaningfulness, it's easy to dismiss the notion that work can be a source of meaning in our lives.

It's no surprise that meaning at work is easily disregarded; organizations around the globe suffer from chronic employee dissatisfaction and disengagement, toxic cultures, and demotivating work climates. It's difficult to find meaning in such conditions. With the recent Great Recession in America and the financial global crises that started in 2007, people have grown disillusioned and dismayed with executive and government power players. These power players caused the financial crises, which fueled wider-spread malaise in workplaces. Employees have grown weary and want to feel something that moves them. They are tired of feeling angry, ignored, undervalued, and overworked for 2 percent pay increases while CEOs and their direct reports continue to earn large salaries and bonuses despite underperformance.

In search of something contrary to what ails the workplace, leaders turn to lists heralding the unique few who can make great places work. Perhaps embedded in the write-ups of such companies are nuggets of inspiration that give hope and provide a glimpse of what could be useful in making the workplace more tolerable. While I applaud and am grateful for the hard work by the companies that make such lists, what might leaders think about their companies that are not included in the perennial lists? I worry that these leaders conclude it's not possible for their organizations or team to have a little bit of "the goodness" that could improve their workplace environment.

So in response, leaders give up before even trying because the effort seems so daunting. A place to start is in making meaning. It's an antidote to what ails too many workplaces, perhaps yours. Meaning is something you can influence as a steward. It doesn't need to be only at an organizational level. You can help your people, including yourself, find meaning in their work.

> **Stewards use meaning to personalize the work experience.**

Joanna Barsh and her colleagues at McKinsey & Company found that more than 2,000 executives placed finding meaning in their activities as the strongest influencer on life satisfaction.[2] In a DeVry University study, 71 percent of millennials said meaningful work was the top career factor defining success.[3] In a separate report, a sense of meaning was found to be millennials' top career need.[4] In these studies, satisfaction in life or in one's career was not higher pay, though this factor is often confused to be the top motivator. While money is a motivator, its influence is short-lived. We adjust our lifestyles to extra money, resulting in its waning influence over our behaviors.

What the data hint at is meaning's potential influence on employee retention. In the DeVry study, a significant percentage of millennials said they want meaning as part of their employment experience. In this era when employees stay with a company fewer than four years, it would be prudent for leaders to learn how to help people find meaning in their work and have a meaningful work experience.

We all want to be touched, moved, and inspired by life. Meaning is a source not just for life but for work, too. As a steward of unlocking human potential, meaning is an opportunity to turn your people's work efforts and interest into something that matters. Meaningful work is the second element in the Origins of Optimism. It's also your shot at helping people see how their work contributes to a bigger picture and to feel connected to a group of like-minded people.

MEANING AND MEANINGFUL WORK

It doesn't matter if it's meaning or meaningful work, both are a path to humanizing the workplace. The human condition has long been absent in the consideration of most workplaces. We can criticize Google for providing benefits like on-site day-care and laundry services as a way to keep people on its campus and working longer hours. Or we can recognize Google for understanding the sacrifice employees make by giving much of their time to their employer and providing solutions that help employees manage their day-to-day lives more easily. Both are small gestures to help pave the path forward to finding meaning or doing meaningful work.

What's the difference between meaning and meaningful work? Simply speaking, meaning is a personal experience. It's experienced when your team members find significance in their work. It's not the work itself, but the impact it has on the person. Obvious examples would be volunteering for something important to the employee or finding significance in the purpose behind a project.

A steward invests effort to learn how to make work a meaningful experience for her employees: heading up a work committee for an important cause, mentoring a new employee, revising outdated policies, writing code for a pet project. Meaningful work is work that aligns with employees' values, strengths, interests, and talents. Helping employees find meaning and do meaningful work does require you to reset some of your perceptions about how work is assigned to employees. We'll go deeper into this in Chapter 8. For now, what's important to understand is that meaning is not a nice-to-have but an essential element to creating optimism.

Areas of Meaning

It's helpful to think of meaning in three different areas, or what I call Areas of Meaning. The first area is Social. This is where employees find meaning in helping others inside and outside the organization. The second area is Work. Employees need to understand how their efforts support the team's success and the organization's, too. Work needs to facilitate meaning given that it's a dominant focus in our lives. The last area is Personal. This is where meaning is derived from actions employees take to improve their own lives.

MEANINGFUL WORK AND WORKPLACE OPTIMISM

"I want to make things better for people."

"We are responsible for protecting our brand."

"We're going to make sure that when people start, they know that they're special."

"I recognize people [who] haven't been recognized."

"I think caring environments are high-accountability environments."

"My purpose is to connect with people [here at work]."

"I'm a better person because I work here."

"Witness and be part of people who are really proud and excited about what they're doing or what they've accomplished."

This is what meaning sounds like. In optimistic climates, meaning transforms the interactions between people; there's a familial feel to interactions. People want to be around each other. The history between people and groups or teams is held with positive regard. Meaning can be experienced from the good times, as reflected in the quotes above. However, meaning can also be experienced from difficult times that bring people together. Meaning and meaningful work have a lasting impression on us. Meaning becomes folded into the interactions you and your team have that elevate everyone to higher levels of self-awareness and performance.

Workplace optimism is how employees feel about the environment. When at work they feel hopeful, believe that good things are possible. To that end, meaning and meaningful work contribute to this perception of workplace optimism. The reason for the focus on meaning is its enduring qualities and positive influence on helping people live up to their potential.

Researcher Roy Baumeister and his colleagues researched the lasting effects of meaning on people's lives. They found that meaning goes beyond the present moment and is experienced when people also reflect on the past and anticipate the future. This temporal shifting illuminates the long-term influence meaning plays in our lives.[5] For stewards, Baumeister's work provides several invaluable insights. First, since meaning is based on a person's perceptions of the environment, you need to remain aware of your employees' hopes and needs. Your goal is to stay informed about how your team perceives the work environment and learn what can shift it to be or remain positive. Learn what helps the team members experience meaning or what detracts from it. Second, positively influencing the environment needs diligent focus from you. Optimistic climates are not an assumed reality, nor are employees who find meaning in and through their work. Finally, give your team hope that the climate will become or remain optimistic. If the future is hopeful, it leads your team members to conclude that the climate will be better and they can find meaning, even if it's not currently present.

Actions to Help Meaning Emerge

The dancing panda mascot of BambooHR, a young company outside Salt Lake City, Utah, is a sight to see, with its big head and long body. BambooHR makes an HR software solution for businesses growing in human resources complexities. What interested me about the company is its antiworkaholic policy. Certainly it's a plus in terms of morale, and besides that it plays a significant influence on meaning. Let's look at actions you can take as a steward to help meaning emerge at work. We'll start with the benefits of BambooHR's antiworkaholic policy:

❏ *Focus on how work can positively influence employees' family life and health.* BambooHR's antiworkaholic policy is a nice way to strongly nudge employees to get their work done in 40 hours. That, however, is not the reason for its creation. The start-up's cofounders, Ben Peterson and Ryan Sanders, want employees to have time for their families and participate in activities that bring them happiness. The belief is that if family needs are tended to, employees will be better able to focus on doing great work. It's a mutually beneficial arrangement. Peterson and Sanders have the antiworkaholic policy because it aligns with their core values—organizationally and personally. In fact, a trend across all the companies I studied for this book was the positive influence work had on an employee's family and personal life. The positive perceptions this created about the workplace climate are significant. Employees expressed gratitude and experienced greater fulfillment outside work. Research backs up what these two entrepreneurs are doing. Italian professor Antonella Delle Fave and her team repeatedly found that family and close relationships were the most meaningful source of psychological happiness.[6] This is the type of happiness that is fulfilling and lasting. This is the opposite of fleeting happiness, like what you experience when you buy a new car. That excitement eventually wears off and stops being a constant source of happiness. BambooHR is serious about ensuring that employees have time for family and interests outside work. It's not uncommon for newly hired employees to express surprise and comment on how happy they are that work doesn't interfere with spending time with their significant others: "I love being home with my family. . . . My husband knows I'm happy; my kids know I'm happy." Employees have found deeper enjoyment for their work and in their interests in life.[7] The inherent respect BambooHR has for employees' whole life—personal and professional—magnifies employees' appreciation for their manager and the company. Ryan Sanders of BambooHR insightfully asked me why leaders would want to be responsible for contributing to a negative personal life because of work's dominance.

❏ *Learn and leverage employees' strengths.* Strengths are not what your employees are good at—they are what energizes them. According to Gallup research, the more hours people use their strengths "to do what they do best, the less likely they are to report experiencing worry, stress, anger, sadness, or physical pain." Again according to Gallup, those who use their strengths 10 hours or more a day experience less worry, stress, and those other emotions listed.[8] Ten hours may seem like a long time. Strengths, however, don't only apply to work. They count when employees use their strengths outside work, too. This is further reason why it's important to help employees find the right mixture of time working and spending time with family. (As a side note, family is whatever a person defines it to be. For some, family can be a spouse and children; for others, it can be just a significant other.) Finally, how employees feel about the work environment is directly linked to perceptions of their boss. While this isn't new insight, it serves as a valuable reminder and it positions learning how to leverage employees' strengths as one way to have a connected relationship with them. It makes sense to leverage employees' strengths to help them grow. When you help employees grow, you increase the meaning they feel from their work.

❏ *Prevent moral bankruptcy.* Meaning is strangled by morally bankrupt leadership actions. Without exception, these actions reflect 20th-century management practices such as profit-first or shareholder-value-first perspectives, overly short-term thinking, self-interested actions, or unbending viewpoints on the leader's role to shape the culture and climate. Financial decisions are made without significant consideration of the implications for people. The manufacturing company Barry-Wehmiller faced having to lay people off for financial reasons. CEO Bob Chapman presented the predicament to employees. Collectively, they decided to cut their hours and take unpaid vacations to avoid laying people off. It worked. The collaborative effort between leaders and employees prevented layoffs. It also helped the company maintain its strong relationship with employees.[9] Too often, when organizations face financial pressures, leaders take the easiest and most familiar path: Reduce the workforce. What Chapman's company showed is that the proverbial wisdom of the crowd prevails: Collectively, the crowd knows the solution to a problem.

❏ *Express genuine appreciation to employees.* In my work with clients, a lack of expressed appreciation from leadership is a common concern employees have. According to a study by Ken Blanchard Companies, an environment that is safe, open, and welcoming is what makes a company a special place to work.[10] This is an outcome of expressing appreciation to employees. Think of a time when you worked hard on something for your boss and received no acknowledgment. Sure, it's your responsibility to do your best work. Yet the appreciation signals your boss cares. Without the expression of appreciation, you are likely to become ambivalent toward what good work is, what it means, or if your work is acceptable or could improve. Researcher Barbara Fredrickson says appreciation is a positive emotion that can leave people feeling safe and satisfied. Furthermore, "positive emotions have a complementary effect. They broaden people's momentary thought-action repertoires, widening the array of thoughts and actions that come to mind."[11] When you express appreciation, it inspires others to do the same; it's leadership karma: Do something positive for someone and she will likely do the same.

In fact, according to Fredrickson's research, positive emotions promote a person's development. "By experiencing positive emotions, individuals can transform themselves, becoming more creative, knowledgeable, resilient, socially integrated, and healthy." Individuals who regularly experience positive emotions continually grow toward optimal functioning. Certainly appreciation drives more than positive emotion. Her research has found it is also linked to joy, hope, gratitude, interest, inspiration, even the *l* word: *love*.[12] Employees want to know that they are valued and not some number built into the salary line in the company's balance sheets. From Fredrickson's work alone, we can see that expressing appreciation can significantly influence the depth and strength of relationships with employees. Employees are key partners in the success of the team and ultimately in the organization. Ben Peterson, CEO of BambooHR, models genuine appreciation in a notable way. He tailors his expression of appreciation to the person. BambooHR's information technology manager, Jeremy Bowers, wanted to take his wife to a Medieval Times event. As a way to thank Jeremy for his work, Ben and Ryan bought tickets for him. Jeremy was speechless and deeply grateful. This is but one story BambooHR employees told me about how their bosses express appreciation. The focus is on making the recognition intentional and purposeful. The outcome is a deeper relationship with team members.

> *Employees are key partners in the success of the team and ultimately in the organization.*

❏ *Focus on people's potential.* Old-school managers pigeonhole employees into their current role. In contrast, stewards see the potential in people and partner with them to explore it and find new ways to unleash it. The savvy steward recognizes that when a team member's potential is encouraged in his professional life, the effects often spill over into his personal life. I remind you of Kelly from Luck Companies and how his professional development positively shaped his role as a husband. Luck stewards work to help employees know that what they contribute at work is valuable, useful. To focus on each person's potential on your team, spend time meeting with each one to learn about what energizes her. This goes back to the importance of knowing your employees' strengths. Luck Companies turns hard, physical labor into meaningful work by helping its associates be better human beings. In turn, associates give their best back to the organization. It's mutually beneficial. Or as Kare Anderson explains, such an arrangement is rooted in mutuality. Anderson's work in mutuality stresses the importance of focusing first on the other person, then yourself, then how you two can work together for a common interest. The striking nuance in Anderson's work is that she stresses the reverse of what most of us tend to do—focus on our needs first. Unleashing the potential of each of your employees requires you to focus on them first—their interests, needs, hopes, wants, concerns, etc. For example, discuss what your team members' aspirations are. Then explore how their aspirations coincide with your interests as a leader. Finally, map the aspirations to how it will benefit you and them and the action you'll take together. This is what Anderson calls "triangle talk," moving the conversation from a "you," to a "me," to an "us" perspective, in that order.[13] Alice Cabrera of HopeLab put it this way: "What can I give of myself to this organization that would benefit us both?"[14]

❏ Bust "drama triangles." In the late 1960s, psychiatrist Stephen Karpman introduced the notion of the "drama triangle" to explain the complexities of human behavior when it comes to creating drama in our lives, drama in our relationships, and the roles we play in perpetuating it. Drama triangles have three roles: the perpetrator, the victim, and the rescuer.[15] The dynamics work like this: Jane (perpetrator) gives harsh feedback to John (victim), who gets annoyed and tells his friend Mark (rescuer) how upset he is with Jane. Mark decides to let Jane know she upset John. Now the roles shift in this drama triangle. Mark becomes the perpetrator and Jane becomes the victim. Jane is now faced with a couple of options. She can go to John and discuss the problem. She can also go tell her colleague Tina what Mark said, creating a new drama triangle. The problem with this all-too-familiar scenario started when John didn't tell Jane that her feedback was upsetting him. The drama triangle wouldn't have started if John had had the courage to speak up and say how he was feeling. The drama started when John went to Mark. Mark could have "busted" the drama triangle from going further by sending John back to talk with Jane. Drama triangles undermine productivity, fuel gossip, and prevent relationships from forming or deepening. The drama distracts people from experiencing meaning in their work or finding work meaningful. Stewards establish a behavioral expectation by constantly sending back the person in the victim role to talk with the perpetrator.

❏ *Be accountable for yourself.* Perhaps the most important action in this list is holding yourself accountable for your commitments. Jim Kouzes and Barry Posner, authors of the book *The Leadership Challenge,* call this DWYSYWD: Do what you say you will do.[16] This establishes credibility, shows consistency in your actions, and ultimately builds trust.

❏ *Champion values alignment.* How do you know if your behaviors and attitudes align with the company's? Just as important, do your behaviors and attitudes align with your personal values? While many organizations make values a marketing tool, stewards live by them. Furthermore, stewards know their personal values and do a values audit regularly. That's when you review your values and ask how you've modeled them in your behavior. When you check yourself for alignment, you become a values champion. Stewards don't use values as a rah-rah approach to leadership. They live by the values and expect others to do so.

The items listed above are the often-overlooked actions you can take as a steward to help meaning emerge at work. Other important actions include giving timely and motivating feedback, connecting people's work to the bigger picture, and providing professional development opportunities for your team.

Making Work Meaningful

While you can't make work meaningful for employees, you can create the conditions for it. Meaningful work can become a source of joy in employees' lives. Max DePree, former CEO of Miller Furniture, says in his book *Leadership Is an Art,* "Work should be and can be productive and rewarding, meaningful and maturing, enriching and fulfilling, healing and joyful."[17] Chip Conley, founder of Joie de Vivre hotels, says in his book *Peak,* "Finding meaning in one's work—both in what you do daily and in the company's sense of mission—is one of the rarest but most valuable qualities anyone can have in their job."[18] Meaningful work can become a calling—not just a job you do Monday through Friday, 9 to 5. Conley is correct in saying that not everyone will find meaning in his work. Yet meaning is central to the efforts of unleashing human potential and, thus, to workplace optimism. More people at every level of an organization, no matter its size, deserve the opportunity to uncover the deeply gratifying feeling that stems from meaningful work. You play a pivotal role in this opportunity. Your part is to help shape the context for meaningful work to emerge. It's important to know how to make work meaningful so you can fulfill your role as a meaning maker. Let's look at the key actions of meaning makers:

❑ *Meet people's basic needs.* In Abraham Maslow's hierarchy of needs (mentioned in Chapter 3), you help employees meet their physiological and safety needs by paying them enough to have a roof over their heads and food on their tables.[19] In terms of how employees perceive the climate at work, safety needs are key: Do employees feel secure in their work? Are expectations clear? Is there consistency in how you show up as a leader? Are your expectations of people clear and consistent? These are basic needs employees expect to be met. If they are not, their absence becomes a distraction and adversely influences how employees perceive you and the environment. Consequently, meaningful work may be difficult to achieve. When basic needs are met, your team members can shift their focus to higher levels of functioning, helping them to do their work better, experience higher levels of happiness, and uncover meaning in what they do.

❑ *Make room for autonomous work.* Researchers Richard Ryan and Edward Deci say being motivated "means to be moved to do something. . . . Someone who is energized or activated toward an end is considered motivated." Based on their research, all people want and need autonomy to be motivated.[20] Carol Ryff found the same to be important in her research. A deeper look at autonomy reveals that we all want to contribute to something important, bigger than ourselves. We want to achieve such outcomes by figuring out how best to do it. When industrial-era mindsets in management prevail, the command-and-control manager fails to see the humanity in his role. There is no emphasis placed on employees' needs to make a difference through their work. Today, having autonomy means team members can rely on their experiences and use their ideas to leave their mark. The intrinsic motivation inherent in autonomy is a source of fulfillment and helps employees find meaning.

❏ *Invite people to be in on things.* Too many organizations suffer from the death of clear communications. The causes? Too much bureaucracy, hierarchy that hinders timely progress, inadequate communication channels, and stifling silos. Employees want to believe they are in on decisions and hear news in a timely manner. When it doesn't happen, the rumor mill becomes the reliable source for information. Trust is negatively impacted. Meaningful work becomes a remote possibility. An excellent example that transcends the causes of unclear communications is open finances practiced by Zingerman's. Zingerman's is a retailer, restaurant, and deli in Ann Arbor, Michigan, and has practiced open finances for years. Employees are educated on important financials for the business and then involved in regular discussions about the companies' financial health. Employees make decisions about how money is spent in their business area. I visited Zingerman's in 2014. During my visit to their many offices in Ann Arbor, I stopped by the company's training room. Posted in an employee area was a white board displaying the team's financial goals and progress. The trainer showing me around casually explained how she and her peers were responsible for financial metrics. She not only understood them, but could also explain their importance to her team, her department, and the organization. At Zingerman's, transparency is designed into the business. Even partner meetings are open to employees to attend. You may not practice open finances or have the authority to invite employees to management meetings, but you can loop employees in on important ideas and considerations sooner to get their input before decisions are made.

Additionally, you can combat the killing of clear communications by communicating information sooner rather than later.

❏ *Give people the freedom to express themselves.* Rosa Lopez is the office manager at HopeLab. When I asked her about why the work environment there is positive, she quickly explained the importance of self-expression. In any situation and with any person, employees feel free to express their ideas, concerns, and thoughts. Rosa said this is because people believe the environment is safe. Meaningful work emerges when people know they can share what's on their mind and that a pink slip won't be on their desk the next day, or they won't be made to feel shame for speaking out. A strong steward diligently and intentionally influences the environment so that people aren't afraid to express their ideas.

❏ *Model values-based leadership.* Learn what your employees' personal values are. If they don't know them, have them identify their values using the exercises in this book. I also recommend Luck Companies' app mentioned in Chapter 5. Discuss with your employees how their personal values show up in their work and where they are absent. Have employees compare their personal values to the organization's. Discuss what insights this holds for them. Work becomes meaningful when it is clear how it aligns with what the employee values.

❏ *Hold regular one-on-ones.* At least monthly, discuss employees' progress in achieving their performance goals. Hold employees accountable to their growth commitments. Chapter 11 includes a framework to having one-on-ones designed to support the cultivation of workplace optimism.

These actions are of the highest value in creating an optimistic workplace. By adding them to your stewardship routines, you shift work away from a physical place to one in which employees' strengths and talents can be expressed. The latter is linked to meaningful work; it's an expression of a person's collective experiences transferred into something of value. In the end, we all want to know that what we do is useful. Meaning is born from this.

THE HARD WORK OF MEANING MAKERS

Bamboo Love is contagious. It's a term of endearment BambooHR employees use to describe their hyper focus on making their software easy to use. The logic is much like that of Menlo Innovations. It's a customer service philosophy of a higher order. The hard work is worth the effort because the outcome is meaningful. Bamboo Love is what colors the work with meaning.

What is your motivation to find meaningful work and create the context for your team to discover or more deeply explore it? This isn't a question of carrots and sticks. The motivation is more intrinsic. With that in mind, here are a few prompts to help you uncover what intrinsic motivators impel you to be a meaning maker:

* ✳ What's in it for you to help others find meaning in their work?

* ✳ What in your work could help you achieve your highest potential?

* ✳ How will helping your team align with meaning make your role as a steward more enjoyable?

* ✳ What's in it for your team members to find meaning in their work?

* ✳ How can you help each person on your team achieve her highest potential?

* ✳ Given your answers, what are the underlying motivators that aren't extrinsic in nature?

The importance of meaningful work is difficult to measure because of how personal it is. Some may not find it important at all while others will hold it as key to their work experience. There are 77 million millennials, and they will make up 75 percent of the workforce by 2025.[21] As a cohort, they want meaningful work and a meaningful life. The forward-thinking steward sees the writing on the wall: Meaning will continue to increase in importance over the next 10 or more years. I don't believe the importance of meaning is limited to a generational era. It's a human desire to do something that matters. Millennials are merely forcing the conversation, expecting leaders to understand the implications and then do something about it.

REAPING THE BENEFITS OF DOING GOOD

Finding meaning and doing meaningful work is a reason for employees to stay with an organization. Rare is the team, or organization for that matter, that offers people the opportunity to explore their potential and do good at the same time. At the heart of meaning is one's ability to make something that matters. Even in the work of flipping burgers, one can find meaning. It's not that flipping burgers is someone's calling. What makes meaning so important is its transformative influence on how we work and relate to one another. Making meaning doesn't focus on the outcome of employees' work; it's about the work experience. The most powerful experience is one that helps employees become better human beings.[22]

The uniting influence meaning has on how we work, relate to one another, and realize our potential is the spark that turns ordinary teams into extraordinarily coordinated powerhouses. Here are some benefits for the steward who is willing to do good by being a meaning maker:

❏ *Goal-directed behaviors become the norm.* Because meaning enriches the work experience, people are prone to get involved more deeply in their work and take greater care in doing a great job. Baumeister found that "the pursuit of goals and fulfillments through ongoing involvements and activities that are interlinked" were central to meaningfulness.[23]

❏ *People become flux-life tolerant.* Baumeister also found that meaningfulness provided greater stability in the face of changes, or what he called the "flux of life."[24] Business environments are perpetually in a state of flux. Teams made up of people who can find stability in the face of constant change have a performance advantage over those who deny or resist the realities of change.

❏ *Stewardship contributes to society's sustainability.* Corporate social responsibility is becoming increasingly important to employees. At the organizational level, those who deliberately work to help employees find fulfillment in their efforts are likely to also make lives better in their community or in society.

❏ *Employees achieve laser-focused ambition.* Certainly, making a sale or serving a customer is important to a business's longevity. Without meaning, the impact of this work could be lost to monotony. With meaning, people are more driven to raise their performance. Ambition levels are higher in employees who find meaning in their work.

Meaningfulness is a bright spot in creating workplace optimism. But meaning has little to do with money. It has to do with standing up for something of importance and throwing yourself into its service. While the critics of meaning may say it's nonsensical stuff that has no room in today's workplace, a growing number of people, of all ages, are raising their hand to say, "I want fulfillment from my work." Some of those raising their hands are willing to forgo more money. Meaningfulness isn't just about what you or I experience today. It paves the way for those who come after us to have a work experience that's positive and rewarding.

CHAPTER 8

We Must Change
the Way We Work

*Craft is not a rote, calculated path. It is an explosive, messy,
terrifying, and passionate adventure.*

—PAM SLIM, *BODY OF WORK*

WORK GETS A F.A.I.S.E. LIFT

In today's fragmented marketplaces and hypercompetitive business environments, it is increasingly more important to change the way we work. Organizations respond to these external influences with a sense of urgency that also characterizes the nature of work: Get things done quickly. Deliver results efficiently. Hurry. Hurry. Hurry. The work needed to meet business demands is too often robbed of enjoyment. Despite the impact meaning and purpose has on work, organizations and leaders have been slow to acknowledge their importance and influence. There is hardly enough time to savor the artistry in work. It's buried beneath the rapid pace of getting things done.

Employees are overwhelmed, stressed, burned out, and disillusioned with their ability to positively make a difference through their work. Yet the relationship employees have with work, the pace and quantity of it, and how they achieve desired outcomes is central to cultivating workplace optimism. Leaders need to improve how employees relate to and go about doing their best work. Work today needs a face-lift, or a F.A.I.S.E. lift. F.A.I.S.E. refers to five domains leaders need to address when shifting how employees make sense of the importance of their work, how they approach their work, and ultimately how they generate value for the organization and its customers through their work (see Table 8-1).

The Financial domain may seem to be the odd one among the five. However, it is arguably the most important one in the mix. Without healthy financials, an organization's ability to do innovative, creative work is crippled. Also, employees typically suffer from little opportunity to grow when an organization is underperforming financially, which diminishes the powerful effects of the other four domains. Also important in this domain is leadership's ability to balance short-term and long-term financial perspectives. Too often organizations look to the short term to assess the value of work. For example, shareholder value, often a short-term financial return, is too often considered first before evaluating the long-term value a project might have on the organization.

Table 8-1. The F.A.I.S.E. domains.

Work Domain	Work Domain Description
Financial	Leaders balance long-term and short-term views on financial performance to determine work priorities.
Aspirational	Use of purpose and meaning help bring significance to work and how it's done.
Individual	Leaders leverage work to promote employee self-awareness. Work identity is important.
Social	Employees make sense of work by developing relationships within departments and teams as well as outside the organization.
Environmental	The conditions and climate of the workplace need to bring out employees' strengths and minimize distractions.

The Aspirational, Individual, Social, and Environmental domains more directly influence an employee's relationship with her work. Aspirational, Individual, and Social are often personal for employees, who are the direct beneficiaries. As a steward you have the greatest influence on the Environmental domain. This domain's effects on people are significant, and, I might add, often misunderstood and underestimated.

F.A.I.S.E. Benefits

When attention is given to F.A.I.S.E. domains, you can create a host of organizational benefits. The domains are intended to guide you through how to identify and explain the value of work for both the organization and employees. When work is crafted to promote the Aspirational, Individual, Social, and Environmental domains, it helps increase the meaningfulness of the work. Increased motivation is often attributed to the Aspirational domain; employees want to make a difference in their work and have an impact on others, both sources of intrinsic motivation.[1]

Here's an example of how the presence of the five domains can make a difference. At PepsiCo, a program called Performance with Purpose shapes the work of employees. More than a program, Performance with Purpose is a set of beliefs.

Whether PepsiCo is focusing on human sustainability (Social domain) or talent sustainability (Individual domain), it makes decisions to do good for its customers (Aspirational domain) and those who create the value for the organization—the employees. With a comprehensive set of initiatives—ranging from corporate governance to supply-chain diversity to workplace diversity—PepsiCo positions itself for financial performance.

According to a 2013 PepsiCo report, 89 percent of the company's employees, including executives, feel pride in their work (Environmental domain) and in what the organization accomplishes through its many efforts to improve the communities it serves and create a workplace environment that motivates and inspires employees.[2] With an emphasis on the Financial and Aspirational domains, PepsiCo's CEO, Indra K. Nooyi, keeps her sights on the company's Performance with Purpose to help maintain its competitive advantage. Performance with Purpose is PepsiCo's contract with society.

JOB CRAFTING FOR MAXIMUM IMPACT

The five domains of F.A.I.S.E. serve as a framework to shift the way your employees work. But what does that look like? Professors Amy Wrzesniewski of New York University and Jane Dutton of the University of Michigan propose reshaping relationships, tasks, and how employees think of their work to maximize meaningfulness. Along with The Wharton School of the University of Pennsylvania Professor Justin Berg, they outline an approach to shift the way employees work; it's called job crafting.

Layer F.A.I.S.E. over the job-crafting model and you can change the way your team members work and find greater meaning in what they do and discover more about themselves in the process.

Job crafting is a bottom-up approach that involves employees in the process of shaping what their work looks like. The focus is on three areas: task crafting, relational crafting, and cognitive crafting.

According to Berg, Wrzesniewski, and Dutton, task crafting is when you work with your employees to alter their job responsibilities by adding or eliminating the quantity, scope, and type of tasks. I recommend making these changes with knowledge about employees' strengths—what work energizes and what work drains them. Task crafting also uses meaningfulness as a guide to help employees find significance in their work. An example of task crafting would be to have an employee begin facilitating large group meetings that are key to the company's strategic plan.

Relational crafting is about changing the quality and amount of interaction employees have with others throughout the organization. The focus is on changing how, when, and with whom employees interact when working. Developing and maintaining relationships is central to relational crafting. This is great for exposing employees to other people in business units throughout the organization. Berg, Wrzesniewski, and Dutton give hospital custodians as an example. Rather than focus only on the task of cleaning hospital rooms, some custodians shifted their work focus to include interacting with patients and their families and with visitors. This gave the custodians a greater sense of meaning in their work.

Finally, cognitive crafting focuses on changing how employees make sense of tasks and the relationships necessary to do the work. In a fast-food setting, it's not unrealistic for workers to see tasks as routine and the goal as simply getting customers through the line quickly. Cognitive crafting would help the employee see, for example, that the tasks necessary to get a customer's order correct are essential to satisfying a customer's hunger. And while the customer waits, the employee can make her feel welcome by making small talk.[3]

The value of job crafting to workplace optimism is in its collaborative nature: Employee and manager work together to make alterations to task, relational, or cognitive attributes of work. Employees "get their fingerprints" on work, deepening their ownership of one of the biggest influences on their lives.

F.A.I.S.E. enters the job-crafting conversation in each of the five domains. They can guide your thinking about how to contribute to the conversation with your employee. For example, when task crafting with your employee, the Aspirational domain can help you ask questions about purpose and meaning.

The Individual domain will help you ask questions about an employee's sense of self at work, such as, "How do you view your accomplishments over the past three months?" Going a bit deeper, companies like Aetna have incorporated mindfulness and meditation practices. Such practices help a person increase his self-awareness. Aetna touts benefits, from employees being more present minded to being easier to work with.[4]

WORK PLAYER VERSUS TEAM PLAYER

In our interview, Alice Cabrera of HopeLab distinguished for me the difference between a work player and a team player. A work player is someone who shows up to do the work, does just what's expected with minimal interaction with others, and has little engagement with the workplace. Conversely, a team player is someone who does work collaboratively, builds relationships across the organization and in his team, and goes beyond what's expected. These players see where opportunities are to step up, and they direct their strengths and skills to help the team and to demonstrate their passion. You don't want work players on your assignments or projects; for them, work is merely something to check off a list. You want the passion of team players to identify, plan, implement, and monitor the work needed for results. While employees choose which of the two they want to be, the climate helps shape their choice. This is where your responsibility factors into the work equation.

Team players contribute more than just their skills and strengths. Research from Deloitte's Center for the Edge identifies three attributes for employees it calls explorers. (I view explorers and team players synonymously.) The three attributes are commitment to domain, questing, and connecting.[5]

Commitment to domain is a team player's drive to deepen her knowledge in a particular business domain. These employees remain in what I call wisdom loops, a constant learning and growth cycle that contributes tremendous value to the team and the organization, and is satisfying for the employee. "Commitment to [d]omain helps individuals focus on where they can make the most impact," say the researchers from Deloitte.[6] This is where purpose and passion come together. The powerful combination is what keeps team players engaged in their wisdom loop and "constantly seeking lessons and innovative practices" from other domains.

The questing attribute, or inclination, is marked by a proactive, curious exploration of one's work even if it takes the team player outside his core responsibilities. The type of work it is plays an important role. It needs to be challenging and align with the team's and organization's purpose. This is the fundamental shift in how leaders view the work their people do. Rather than focusing on assignments, stewards create the conditions that give their employees the room to explore and be curious. Additionally, stewards take the time to learn what the domain's expert skills are for their team

> *Stewards create the conditions that give their employees the room to explore and be curious.*

members. This insight is leveraged to position the team for creating maximum impact through its work. But the benefits go deeper than results.

The work becomes deeply gratifying for team members. Work becomes art.[7] Not art as in a painting, but the finesse a person shows in connecting the intention and outcomes of the work to the people who will benefit from it. No longer is the work done for some faceless end user. It's created with passion, intention, and delight for a customer who has a personal history, needs, hopes, and dreams. In short, today's employees, or team players, want to create something that can be offered up, as if to say, "Look, I made this for you."

The final attribute of Deloitte's explorers is connection. This is simply an employee's relationship-building skills. Just as Berg, Wrzesniewski, and Dutton advocated for relationship building in their job-crafting model, Deloitte's Center for the Edge research also highlights its importance. In the next chapter I'll explore more deeply the importance of relationship building, or connection.

For work to be an artistic expression, it's important to find ways to reframe how you view it. Work is not something to be assigned. In all its beauty and complexity, work is a personal expression stamped by the expertise, experiences, and education—formal and/or informal—of each person on your team. This requires that you link outcomes to strengths and passions, domain expertise, exploration and curiosity, and connection.

THE ORIGINS OF OPTIMISM REVISITED

The optimistic workplace doesn't follow a people-first philosophy. It's rooted in the belief that purpose shapes the work that attracts and depends on extraordinary people. Instead of a people-first philosophy, it's a purpose-centric mindset that is paramount to the optimistic workplace.

That's not to say that people aren't important. An organization is nothing without people. It is merely a set of processes, systems, and technologies. These are only brought to life by the efforts of people. But the force that shapes what people focus on is purpose.

As a steward, you are an evangelist of purpose. You are a preacher of purpose. Without purpose, the work is baseless and lacks a targeted outcome. So it is with intention that you help link purpose to the *how* and *why* of work.

A MODERN VIEW OF WORK

Arcane beliefs about how work is done undermine people's potential. They are rigid; box people in by role; and discount passions, strengths, and skills. In a 2014 study by The Jensen Group about the future of work, one participant from the technology company SAP succinctly summarized the new philosophy about the workplace: "We have to start thinking not about fitting people into jobs, but rather looking at the person and creating a job around them, nurturing their passions and developing their skills."[8]

Given the prevalent stand that people must sacrifice their interests for the good of the organization, the opposite seems heretical. Bill Jensen, the founder of The Jensen Group, explains that people will only stay if the organization creates an environment that allows "the worker to explore his/her passions and push them further."[9] Trends are emerging that support this shift away from a sacrifice-your-needs-to-the-organization mentality to an arrangement that benefits both the company and its employees. Research is also helping us better understand the influence work has on our personal relationships and the effect those relationships have on our work.

> *Trends are emerging that support this shift away from a sacrifice-your-needs-to-the-organization mentality to an arrangement that benefits both the company and its employees.*

Work-Life Mix: A Unified Perspective

Romance and intimacy hold curious insights about your work-life mix. For centuries, organizations have put into place human resources practices and followed management philosophies that unnaturally advocated for employees to separate their personal lives from their professional ones. Research from Germany by Dana Unger and her colleagues reveals that when it comes to our relationship with our significant other, the two worlds do collide and cannot be easily separated.[10]

Through daily online diary entries, Unger had research participants answer questions and respond to statements in the morning, after work, and just before going to bed. The questions and statements were aimed at helping the researchers measure the quality of the relationship and understand the hassles couples experience. Statements participants agreed or disagreed with included, "This morning, my relationship with my partner makes me happy" and, "Yesterday evening, my partner was impatient." Work-related questions included, "How long did you work today?" and, "How long did you work this evening?" Even prompts about intimacy and support were explored: "Yesterday evening, my partner shared something personal or private" or, "Yesterday evening, my partner was supportive of me."[11]

What Unger and colleagues learned was somewhat counter to the popular belief that as a way to escape, we will bury ourselves in our work when problems occur at home. This is not what researcher Dana Unger and her colleagues found. Through the diary entries, they found that when times were difficult at home, a partner's work suffered, even if she was attempting to distract herself from the problems. "Indicators of poor relationships were associated with less time spent on work."[12]

Here we have a dilemma. Often leaders will avoid discussing emotional and personal circumstances in an employee's life. Such conversations can be taboo. Unfortunately, avoiding them leaves the leader wondering why her employee is falling behind. Without inquiring into what's going on with the employee, wrong conclusions may be reached.

The German researchers also found that relationships with low degrees of hassles resulted in partners making more of their time available for work.

That second finding is compelling. It raises the question of whether organizations should provide more than employee-assistance programs to support the quality of their employees' overall work-life mix. Unger's research doesn't suggest such an offering, but it's compelling enough for consideration. Should leaders discuss employees' personal lives with them because it affects their performance at work? I believe so. To downplay the impacts of employees' personal lives on their work—and vice versa—leaves the door open to unexplored influences on performance. The team is impacted, and so, too, is project work or other assignments.

Tying Unger's and her team's results to Carol Ryff's psychological well-being work, a powerful insight emerges: An organization can help elevate employees' self-acceptance and personal growth by providing support or resources that deal with resolving relationship issues that aren't work related. The business case for this can be made by looking to resolve performance issues that stem from low-quality and high-hassle personal relationships. Stewards can provide guidance on finding resources that can address problems at home, such as counseling on money matters or caring for elderly parents.

A deeper look at the work implications of Unger's research reveals that employees' perception of the work experience can be negatively impacted by personal relationship hassles. Employees who experience unhealthy levels of stress fall behind at work; their work quality suffers, and so do work relationships. Perceiving the climate as one marked with optimism is less likely when the work-life mix is troubled. While you cannot solve a troubled employee's personal problems, you can be part of the solution to help her resolve them so she can get back to leveraging her strengths and passions for organizational benefit.

WORK TRENDS THAT INFLUENCE THE OPTIMISTIC WORKPLACE

Organizations today are influenced by many variables, including social changes, technology advances, economic ups and downs, and political and legal matters. The porous organization is in a constant state of change and transition from one way of doing things to a new one. Certainly your organization's culture helps or hinders its abilities to change. Yet culture change is difficult and takes a long time. But by focusing on creating an optimistic workplace, you have greater influence on your team's abilities to adapt to the forces of change.

Your employees' quality of life is at stake, too, according to research by Stanford University's Jeffrey Pfeffer, Ph.D. As a major social influence on the workplace, unhealthy work environments cost the United States $130 billion and cause 125,000 deaths each year, Pfeffer estimates. Some of the factors that impact the data are within a steward's control or influence to change. For example, Pfeffer's research shows when employees have no control over their work, their stress levels are affected. Paid overtime, while helpful financially, can impact quality of sleep and disrupt the work-family mix.[13]

The Great Place to Work Institute, the organization that creates *Fortune* magazine's list of 100 Best Companies to Work For, shows us that the best workplaces have a positive impact on their employees and counter the ill health effects caused by some of the common workplace maladies. For example, among employees working at the 2014 Fortune 100 Best Companies to Work For, 77 percent believe management involves them in decisions that give them control over their work. Other interesting trends emerge from the institute's data: 87 percent of employees in these great companies feel a sense of family or team at work; 83 percent believe they are encouraged to balance their work and personal lives. (I don't believe in the concept of balance. Balance implies tradeoffs and leads us to pursue an equilibrium that's just not possible in today's world. You may have noticed I use the term *work-life mix* or *integration*. It captures the reality that we all work to integrate the various roles in our lives in some coherent manner that works for us, no matter how messy it may be.) Finally, of those companies listed in the best places to work, they cover 60 to 100 percent of full-time employees' health insurance premiums. Of those, 91 percent cover 60 to 100 percent of dependent health premiums.[14]

Though *Fortune*'s 100 Best Companies to Work For list features organizations that have a fully coordinated effort to improve the workplace environment, there are lessons for you that can be mapped to your effort to improve your team's climate to be optimistic. For example, you can work with your employees to give them control over how they do their work through job crafting and using the F.A.I.S.E. domains. When you intentionally create a positive climate, you begin to influence the sense of family or team. You can model boundary setting to ensure that your personal life is not neglected because of work commitments. Think BambooHR and its antiworkaholic philosophy.

Let's look at some of the key trends that are influencing the workforce today. By responding to them proactively, you can leverage their influence to help employees believe that where they are—on your team—is exactly where they want to be.

There's a strong argument that these trends need to be addressed at the organizational level. You'll get no argument from me on that point. However, what I'm more interested in right now is helping you to create a pocket of excellence. You can positively shape the work experience to be optimistic for your people. Let people within the organization learn about the great things you're doing for your team. Others will come and inquire into what you're doing because the results will speak for themselves.

There are many trends that we could focus on here. I'm limiting them by focusing on those trends that you can likely implement with little to no approval. I intentionally leave out trends like BYOD (bring your own device). This typically requires changes to information-technology infrastructure, policies, and business practices. My goal is to help you be a more-engaged steward with your employees' growth, well-being, and overall work experience. And this starts with focusing on microchanges that are often within a leader's control or influence. The work trends below are categorized two ways: workforce expectations and views on work.

Workforce Expectations Shaping How We Work

Employees see organizations as a way to achieve their goals and dreams.[15] Without work, they cannot easily fulfill their passions or achieve their goals. Work is a source of fulfillment when the steward provides opportunities that help people advance in their careers. This perspective hasn't always been the case. Millennials are pushing organizations to modernize their business practices related to workforce expectations.[16] These are the areas employees view as critical to their work life:

❏ *Advancement.* It's common to hear remarks about the unrealistic expectations millennials have about advancing in the organization without doing the time. After all, that's what previous generations had to endure. So that's the way it ought to be, right? No. It is human nature, not generational characteristics, that impels us to seek out opportunities to better our current station in life. Notable Stanford University psychologist Albert Bandura says, "The capacity to exercise control over the nature and quality of one's life is the essence of humanness."[17]

It's a mental shortcut and trap to conclude that how things were for you is how they need to be for others. We must account for the forces of change on how things are done today. It is no longer best practice to assume experience is the major factor for career advancement. What matters now are drive, character, values, and potential.

One need look only as far as government to see that length of time in a position is not a good measure for promoting people. Government is notorious for promoting people who have "done the time" but lack the drive, character, values, or potential. This sets people up for frustration and failure that can lead to adverse health effects on the person promoted. Furthermore, team performance takes a hit. For optimism to emerge, people at all ages must have the opportunity to advance because they demonstrate that they are ready or show great potential.

LinkedIn uses a tour-of-duty concept to intentionally develop employees' skills that help them achieve their career aspirations. A tour of duty could yield valuable benefits, like an expanded professional network or a newly learned skill. The tours are rooted in a mutually beneficial belief that Reid Hoffman and his coauthors outline in *The Alliance*.

The alliance referred to in the book is a relational perspective with a focus of ensuring the business and the employee get to desired outcomes that are important to both. Employees might embark on a rotational, transformational, or foundational tour of duty. The approach is embedded in LinkedIn's culture.[18] You could implement such an approach internally with your team or partner with other managers in other business areas.

❏ *Coaching and/or Mentoring Relationships.* Whether it be junior- or senior-level employees, support for their growth is central to the optimistic workplace. You can show this support by making coaching or mentoring available to help your people grow in their work, even their personal lives. Show that you care about your employees' well-being and successes. A quick note about the difference between coaching and mentoring. Coaches will use a questioning tactic to help those they are coaching discover the answer to meet their needs. For example, I was coaching a manager who was a workaholic and considered an unpleasant person. Her expectations for others were unrealistic. She worked around the clock, and there was an unspoken expectation that her team should, too. When I asked her what was missing from her life because of her work schedule, she said golf. So we put into place a plan that allowed her to play more golf. In addition to being her coach, I became her accountability partner, helping her stick to her plan to find time for play in her life. It was the timing of my question that helped the manager begin to unravel her problem so she could make room to play golf with friends with whom she had lost touch. Mentoring is a bit more directive. The mentor might not use the art of questioning to help the mentee. The mentor may direct the mentee to do something and then review the action later. I have a mentor who helped me hone my public speaking. She gave me assignments that I needed to complete and then I reviewed my work with her in the next mentoring session.

❏ *Work Flexibility.* Ninety-one percent of the employees on the *Fortune* list of best companies to work for said they believe they can manage their own work schedules to get work done and tend to personal needs as they arise.[19] This is one form of flexibility that you can incorporate into your philosophy of stewardship. Work flexibility also includes letting people work where they want to. One of my government clients rolled out a program that allows employees to work remotely once a week. Other organizations let employees work remotely all the time. This type of flexibility lets your people match their energy levels optimally. Some employees are morning people. Work flexibility lets them choose hours that help them be most productive. Jeffrey Pfeffer's research showed that when employees have control over their work, they can flex more easily when and where it is done.[20] This doesn't mean deadlines and milestones are not expected. Work flexibility is only successful when rigor around execution is part of the conversation. Harvard Business School professor Teresa Amabile and her coauthor Steven Kramer explained in their book *The Progress Principle* that when people experience progress in their work, they are more engaged in what they're doing.[21] Work flexibility provides employees with the opportunity to make progress on their work.

❏ *Social Responsibility.* Businesses have a responsibility to improve the communities where they operate. Barry-Wehmiller CEO Bob Chapman believes that "business could be the most powerful force for good if it embraces the responsibility and impact [it can] make on people's lives."[22] Businesses have the resources and influence to make positive changes at local and even global levels. Employees play a significant part in this noble belief. Millennials are pushing this conversation to newer levels. In one study focusing on this generation, job satisfaction was linked to volunteering and working on a project that helps society or the environment. In the same study, 65 percent of those responding said contributing to society was an important job attribute.[23]

These trends provide insight into how you can partner with your employees to help them direct their passion into their work. Other trends that are important to employees and influence their work include meaningful and purposeful work and a sense of community. Chapter 10 goes deeper into creating community.

These trends provide you the opportunity to show you care about employee well-being and success. Stewardship is about getting things done. Equally as important, however, is the recognition that work significantly influences our lives. It shapes the conversations your employees have at home. It influences your people's long-term plans. You get to play a positive part in this when you no longer see work as something to be assigned and crossed off a to-do list.

Pulling Leader Levers to Shift How We Work

Creating a positive work experience is a central goal for stewards. With the above trends in mind, there are some levers you can pull to realize this outcome. Each of the five levers listed in Table 8-2 represents a shift in how we view work. Each one represents a fundamental shift away from a traditional approach to how work is accomplished to one that is optimism building: purpose and meaning; community building and belonging; self-development and self-awareness; values-centered actions and impact; hope and exploration.

Table 8-2 shows a comparison of traditional work levers used to create value for the organization to those that build optimism. The primary driver of traditional views is that the organization is most important. The importance of people is minimized.

To illustrate the point, I recall a TEDx Talk Bob Chapman tells. It's a compelling story of once seeing people as a function, or what they did in his company. He told me he once believed that as long as a person fulfilled his function at work, things were good. Chapman had an epiphany at a friend's wedding when he realized that people aren't functions. This struck him as he watched the bride's father give away his daughter to his future son-in-law. The shift for Chapman came when he realized that the tradition of the father giving his daughter away in marriage was about changing lives. He recounted suddenly understanding that the bride is someone's daughter and is deeply loved. It wasn't about the ceremony, but about the people. In Chapman's TEDx Talk he concludes, "When we allow somebody to walk in to our organization we have an obligation as stewards of that life to continue to allow that life to be everything they were meant to be."[24]

Table 8-2. **Work levers.**

Traditional Work Levers	Optimism-Building Work Levers
Strong organizational focus minimizes personal incentive and focuses on exchange of money for time—transactional.	Purpose and meaning give work focus and significance and reinforce connection between people and work—relational.
Silos and turf wars reinforced by rigid hierarchy limit scope of work.	Community building and belonging unite people and shape work assignments to be diverse and fulfilling.
Time on job and role are main determinants of professional development goals; work-only focus limits self-awareness.	Self-development goals promote growth in how one thinks, feels, and acts; support for whole-employee self-awareness.
Impersonal, vague values are forgotten and have little to no impact on people, community, work, and results.	Values-centered actions evoke passion for work and are intended to maximize impact on people, community, work, and results.
Work and its outcomes are safe and business value is safe or mediocre.	Hope and exploration invite curiosity and innovation to work; outcomes are exceptional and advance team and organizational purpose; greater business value is created.

Chapman's sudden insight reveals a powerful lesson for all stewards: Learning people's stories helps you transcend the viewpoint that employees fulfill functional roles in which they perform perfunctory tasks in exchange for pay. When we fail to do this, we take on a traditional view of work. Consequently, work outcomes are safe, predictable, and hold back teams and ultimately the organization.

Optimism-building views look at work through a relational lens and seek mutually beneficial outcomes for the team, organization, and individual. Another significant difference is placed on each team member's development as a whole person—growth is a focus both personally and professionally.

For the purpose and meaning leader lever, your role is to ensure that the team's purpose is known and how it aligns with the company's goals. Let people choose assignments that align with their strengths—what energizes them—and their development goals. Build community and belonging by intentionally creating meaningful relationships with your team and connecting its members to one another and to their collaborators across the organization. Build dependency between team members by cross-pollinating knowledge on all projects the team is assigned. This is what Menlo Innovations does by rotating people weekly from project to project. This helps keep enthusiasm for the work high by leading people to value constant learning. It promotes hope by taking work and connecting it to purpose.

Curiosity is evoked when you allow your team members to explore new ways to approach their work. Take a page from Google's playbook and set aside time for your team to develop side projects that could someday add value to the organization.

How we work is changing. It's technology driven. It's socially driven. It's purpose driven. These are the shifts that help you connect purpose and meaningful work successfully. The Origins of Optimism fall apart if work is viewed through the familiar, mundane lens that currently dominates most workplaces. Help your people see their work as the pursuit and fulfillment of purpose.

CHAPTER 9

Human-Centered Leadership

Perhaps because we live in a society that markets and hawks the fruits of our labor and not the labor itself, we have forgotten or never really appreciated the fact that the business of work is not simply to produce goods, but also to help produce people.

—AL GINI, *WORK IDENTITY AND SELF*

THE QUEST FOR SOMETHING MORE MEANINGFUL

When I interviewed employees for this book, the first question I asked was, "What makes your heart sing?" I thought it was the best question to help me quickly get a glimpse of what moves people. Here's what Luck Companies CEO Charlie Luck said: "What was haunting me was that there has to be more to life than this. There has to be more to it than just another acquisition or just another new product launch. And not that those things aren't important—they are, but for me, it wasn't totally fulfilling. There's got to be more meaning to life than adding another zero. So what is a lasting difference? What impact can you have on human beings? A lot of things happen through the interaction of human beings. If we can improve human beings' ability to positively exist, work together in a way that's way more productive, then to me, we've left a huge gift. That's what makes my heart sing."[1]

Throughout our conversation, he moved from one relational story to another, genuinely touched by the quality and depth of the relationships in his life. He felt as much joy for the relationships as for their influence on people's lives. "Our most powerful work," he said, "is the impact on people, most importantly to me, away from work, and also at work, but most importantly away from work." In Charlie Luck's wisdom, there is a powerful leadership lesson that transcends title and place: relatedness.

Relatedness is when we have satisfying, trusting relationships with others. We care about the well-being of people and the nuances of give-and-take that are so fundamental to healthy relationships. When we have positive relationships with others we can empathize with them during the difficult times and celebrate in the best of times. Luck Companies, Barry-Wehmiller, Menlo Innovations, Zingerman's, and the many other organizations featured here have successfully integrated a relational attentiveness in their workplaces. Relational attentiveness is a leader's intentional focus on creating a climate that promotes relationship building. Such leaders place a high priority on positive relationships with employees and colleagues.

Researchers are beginning to understand the physiological effects relatedness has on people and its benefits to the organization. One study proposes that positive relationships can help people manage stress levels more effectively, navigating the stressors of work with greater success. The researchers also note that work recovery—an employee's ability to recover from a day's work stressors while at home—also benefits from relatedness.[2]

> *Relationships are an answer to the yearning for something more than a transactional exchange of time for money.*

In a recent conversation I had with an executive, she expressed dissatisfaction with a team of consultants. She wasn't concerned about the quality of work but about late-night emails and the appearance of physical fatigue in some of the consultants. This executive understands that the consulting team's performance will be diminished if its members maintain a late-night work routine. I talked with one of the consultants, who was moved by the concern. She told me that the relationship between the executive and her strengthened in that moment.

Relationships are an answer to the yearning for something more than a transactional exchange of time for money. The newer arrangement is this: In exchange for talents and time, you get money, fulfillment, joy, and the opportunity to become a better human being. A truly human-centered business is one that shakes itself free of the constraints of an Industrial Age mindset, one that dehumanizes people and the relationship between organization and employees.

POCKET OF EXCELLENCE

When I visited Luck Companies in 2014, Charlie Luck and Mark Fernandes both told me, "The organization is the shadow of the leader." I agree with them, though I think the implications of that concept can be concentrated at a more local level, at the team level. Your team is the shadow of you. And in that shadow you can create safety by always building relationships that help people become better human beings. You can create a pocket of excellence no matter what is happening across the organization.

A pocket of excellence is a microcosm within a larger context. No matter what is happening in the larger context, a pocket of excellence is characterized by healthy, productive people who work in an optimistic context. "Whatever standards, values, principles, beliefs the leader exhibits, so goes the organization," explains Charlie Luck. I would add, so goes the team.[3]

> *A pocket of excellence is characterized by healthy, productive people who work in an optimistic context.*

Eighty-five percent of Google employees believe their immediate leader is interested in them as a whole person, not just an employee.[4] This is a key measure for you to monitor in your pocket of excellence. It's an indication that you are having a positive influence on the climate and on the relationships with your team.

IGNORED AND DISILLUSIONED

The relationship with the immediate boss is often a reason employees leave organizations. Unfortunately, connection and belonging are often found with peers only. It is, after all, where the bulk of an employee's time is spent. Certainly, strong peer relationships are important. Yet the relationship between employee and boss is integral to employee growth, satisfaction, and engagement. A study by HR Consulting firm Towers Watson found that the quality of the work experience is linked to the quality of the relationships employees have with their immediate manager and trust in senior leadership.[5] However, only one in three employees believe the relationship with their leader is effective, according to a study by the consulting firm Root.[6] Towers Watson found that 55 percent of employees in its 2014 study indicated that they are inspired by their leader. Additionally, in the same study, only 48 percent of employees believe top leaders are effective.[7] In a different study just 22 percent of employees think leaders have their best interest in mind.[8]

This is an ugly picture; the brushstrokes are familiar, and the results are disappointing. The barriers to fulfilling relationships like those at Luck Companies or Barry-Wehmiller need to be addressed. While it's ideal to start at the top to find solutions to the abysmal state of most workplaces, it's impractical. Improving employees' morale, work engagement, and job satisfaction; changing workplace culture; and addressing work climate issues don't dominate many agendas at the executive level.

To notice what interests your employees isn't a matter of culture. It's a leadership choice. And when it's chosen, it can have powerful implications for optimism in the workplace.

If employees go ignored and their disillusionment is unaddressed, your relationship with them as well as the relationships they have with their peers will continue to be fractured.

As in all relationships, breakdowns go both ways, and both parties have responsibility to address the problem. Employees have a responsibility to identify what their needs are and have conversations about them with their leader. At the same time, leaders need to get used to the shrinking length of time employees spend with an employer and

> *To notice what interests your employees isn't a matter of culture. It's a leadership choice.*

realize that not investing in their potential is a bad choice nevertheless. Creating a climate that helps people explore their potential helps retain people. Employees want to experience a variety of opportunities. Loyalty isn't expressed by staying with a company for a lifetime, but by a person's willingness to grow and give you her best work while she works *with* you. Despite the bleak statistics there is good news: Employees believe the quality of their relationship with you is linked to better days. The question is, what are you willing to do to repair and strengthen the relationship with your team?

THIS IS PERSONAL

The new relationship between you and your staff is no longer judged only by the outcomes it produces. That is archaic thinking, rooted in Industrial Age philosophy, with a core tenet of maximizing output at the expense of people. Some managers in the 19th and 20th centuries didn't believe it was necessary to invest in relationships with people. People were expendable; it was easy to find a willing body to replace someone who wasn't producing the quotas needed to measure financial success and operational efficiencies.

Aetna CEO Mark Bertolini transformed his relationship with employees by offering programs that focus on their health and financial well-being. The focus on well-being resulted from Bertolini's own exploration with alternative health treatments. The CEO had nearly died and was not satisfied with his Western treatment program. Yoga and mindfulness became antidotes to his pain and his path to healthier living, explained author David Gelles in a *New York Times* article.[9]

Bertolini benefited from the practices so much that he offered free yoga classes to Aetna employees. Fifty thousand have taken the course, a quarter of the company's workforce. Benefits attributed to the yoga program are a 28 percent reduction in employee stress levels and 20 percent improvement in sleep quality. Also, 19 percent of employees claim their pain levels are lower. While the goal for Aetna is to improve employees' physical well-being, there are positive relationship side effects, too: The organization is showing that it cares for its employees' health and happiness.

Bertolini also had a positive impact on some employees' financial situations. He increased the lowest-paid employees' incomes by up to a third.[10] Just as the yoga classes offered tangible benefits to the company, this gesture also aided Aetna by helping it keep and attract top talent in a tough labor market. But there are relational benefits, too. Who wouldn't want to give their best to the organization when the top leader shows he cares about people's financial well-being?

Bertolini is a human-centered leader, a leader who places a high value on organizational and people growth. Leaders at Barry-Wehmiller are human centered, too. That company's leadership philosophy is documented in its *Guiding Principles of Leadership*. This internal document boldly proclaims, "We measure success by the way we touch the lives of people."[11]

HopeLab works from a similar philosophy, developing its people to be mature, fully functioning adults by teaching resiliency techniques and self-awareness practices. Rosa Lopez of HopeLab demonstrated the wisdom she's developed by learning how to recognize when she's emotionally triggered by coworkers' actions or words. Before responding, she asks herself, "What triggered me? What happened? Why am I reacting this way?" She told me, "I honestly believe that if you just take that moment or take that breath, you will continue to have this wonderful way of living in this office."[12]

Another company I visited while writing this book is 15Five. Based in San Francisco, California, the software development company also has a human-centered philosophy: "Create the space for people to be their greatest selves."

Human-centered leaders believe that financial success is accomplished through genuinely caring about people. These leaders hold employees accountable to continuously develop their talents so they can advance the company's purpose. But human-centered leaders also want employees to become extraordinary versions of themselves.

HUMAN SIDE OF BUSINESS

Positionally relating to your people means your role precedes your interactions. It's the traditional view of the boss-employee relationship. This relationship style focuses on interactions that center on improving the organization and the sacrifices the employee must make. Employees are expected to fall in line, be obedient, and do what their role requires.

Humanly relating to your people is the evolution of the boss-employee relationship. While the focus does center on improving the organization, it also includes unlocking your people's potential. Employees are expected to anticipate needs, explore alternatives, expand their talents and leverage their strengths, and connect with partners to achieve desired results, not planned results. The marriage of the two—business and human potential—is what the human side of business is about.

What does the human side of business have to do with your relationship with your team? Everything. The human side of business grounds your perspective in truly human elements that help you relate to your team members as people. It guides you to discover commonalities between you and your team that deepen connections. It helps you see where you can make a difference in your people's lives. Such insight is not possible when employees are seen as controllable resources that can't be trusted.

THE UNIVERSAL ELEMENTS OF THE HUMAN SIDE OF BUSINESS

The universal elements of the human side of business are health, family/friends, work, identity, and purpose. The first element, health, includes the physical, psychological, and social health of your people. Towers Watson links these three health types to its measure of well-being. The physical health element focuses on helping people manage their overall health, their energy and stamina levels to live and work. Psychological health has been a significant part of this book's focus, for example, meaning and purpose. Social health is about the quality of relationships people have, the focus of this chapter.[13]

The family/friends element places value on the quality of time your employees have with their family and friends when not at work. It has been found to be most associated with happiness and meaningfulness in life.[14] It's important to note that employees define what *family* means. Today we have our families by birth and also the close circle of friends we create who are viewed as family.

You positively influence the family/friend element by helping employees manage their work-life mix. You monitor use of excessive overtime, though not in a controlling manner. Instead it's to watch for trends that could negatively influence any of the other four elements. You schedule employees for work fairly. You advocate employment practices that help strengthen the family unit, such as maternity/paternity leave and vacation practices. As Charlie Luck and Bob Chapman have learned, when you can strengthen family, employee participation at work strengthens.

The family/friend domain also applies to how your team views itself. The team that works and supports one another is more cohesive. For example, Senior HR Organizational and Associate Development Manager Dawn Hack at Luck Companies told me about employees there who showed support for a grieving coworker who was about to lose his wife to stomach cancer. Employees donated vacation time so he could be with her. The company donated a car and paid for gas so the employee and his wife could spend quality time together traveling before she passed away.[15]

The story is moving. The example is wholly Luck. The lesson isn't in the response but in what facilitated it. Employees believed, and still do, that the quality of their lives is important to the company. This fundamental belief is what makes the actions possible. It's the same belief at BambooHR. The company believes strongly that quality time outside of work is key to a good life.

What can you do to demonstrate the importance of family and friends to improve your employees' quality of life?

In Chapter 8, I discussed why and how work must change. At the heart of this universal element, work, is helping employees find meaning not only in what they do but in the outcomes they help create.

Work shapes our identity. How employees relate to their work self influences their motivation, performance, even job satisfaction. Researchers also find that a healthy work identity helps employees find meaningfulness in their work. These are all important inputs for developing a positive relational attentiveness and cultivating workplace optimism.[16]

The final universal element is purpose. I explored the importance of purpose in Chapter 6, so I won't go into much more detail here. I do want to bring to your attention a thought leader I admire whose work is centered on purpose. Entrepreneur Aaron Hurst, the founder of Imperative, an organization that focuses on helping workplaces be purpose-ful, wrote the following in his book *The Purpose Economy*: "A Purpose Economy is based on empowering people to have rich and fulfilling careers by creating meaningful value for themselves and others."[17] Hurst goes on to explain that this new type of economy is also about service, self-expression, and building community. Purpose, in conjunction with the other universal elements, positions employees to have a remarkable life—personally and professionally.

For ideas on how to apply the universal elements of the human side of business to your situation, see Table 9-1.

Table 9-1. The universal elements.

Human Side of Business Domain	Relationship-Building Actions
HEALTH	**Physical Health** • Provide health benefits. • Offer spouse and domestic partner health coverage. • Offer meditation classes. • Arrange for health-screening events. • Implement a stress-relief program. **Psychological Health** • Help employees discover their personal values. • Provide resources that help employees discover their purpose. • Make coaching and/or mentoring available. • Provide flexible work arrangements. **Social Health** • Make coaching and/or mentoring available. • Implement a job-shadowing program. • Have employees visit other business areas to learn other parts of the company and build a wider network of relationships. • Train employees in conflict management.

(continued)

Human Side of Business Domain	Relationship-Building Actions
FAMILY/FRIENDS	• Monitor employees' overtime; give them time off to be with family in exchange for overtime. • Host after-work dinners with your employees and their significant others. • Celebrate milestones like proposals, weddings, births/adoptions, graduations.
WORK	• Match employees' strengths (what energizes them) to their work assignments. • Job-craft employees' work to promote meaningfulness and work identity. • Ensure employees have assignments that stretch their abilities, which will promote good stress. • Make coaching and/or mentoring available. • Hold regular one-on-ones.
IDENTITY	• Help employees discover their personal values. • Provide resources that help employees discover their purpose. • Make coaching and/or mentoring available.
PURPOSE	• Help employees discover their personal values. • Provide resources that help employees discover their purpose. • Make coaching and/or mentoring available. • Pair up employees to develop a sense of community. • Link interests to work assignments.

ORIGINS OF OPTIMISM REVISITED— EXTRAORDINARY PEOPLE

The human side of business represents the extraordinary people side of business. It's the final element that upholds the Origins of Optimism.

Positive relationships are central to this element. Today's working relationships need to be built on a strong foundation. This includes more deeply knowing who your people are and what they want from their career and out of life.

As it is with any relationship, it takes at least two to believe that the relationship is one that meets everyone's interests. In business, the relationships are between employee and leader, employee and team, and employee and organization. It's ultimately a choice to have a solid relationship. Your employees' decision to choose a relationship with you is more valuable than the economics of the arrangement.[18] It's better to have a vested partner who believes there is value in working together with you. Compare this to having a person on your team who is solely interested in the pay. If an employee merely chooses a paycheck, the economic arrangement is likely short-lived, as pay is often less of a motivator to do good work. However, if an employee chooses a relationship with you, she is committing more deeply to it and going beyond a monetary transaction of pay for knowledge. The choice represents an emotional one that can provide a richer return on her time investment working with you. You benefit from having a more committed team member, a richer partnership, and better-quality work. The relationship serves as a wellspring of possibility for the business, your team, your team member, and you.

There is an inherent trap in looking at a relationship solely as a source of generating business outcomes. Such a view reduces people to resources rather than collaborators or partners. Resources are finite and can be used up and replaced. Laptops, copiers, and money are resources. People have infinite possibilities. You need to create an environment that energizes people and helps them thrive. Relationships are also a source of meaning. That meaning enriches their value and positions relationships to help people feel and think they are part of something bigger than themselves.

> *There is an inherent trap in looking at a relationship solely as a source of generating business outcomes.*

The steward's role is to care for things that don't belong to him. With that in mind, your people don't belong to you. They are free agents. From a stewardship perspective, Bob Chapman summarizes the responsibility of a steward and the care needed for today's work relationships: "Allow everybody to discover, to develop, to share and be appreciated for whatever their gifts are, whatever level they can contribute. It's a privilege and a fundamental obligation of leadership . . . to be a good steward of the lives entrusted to you."[19]

The last part of that quote is intriguing. Chapman has such a strong responsibility for the development of his employees that he views their lives as being entrusted to his care. At the heart of his perspective is seeing the humanity in the relationship, seeing the person. Stanford professor Bob Sutton echoes Chapman's beliefs in an article he wrote for McKinsey, stating, "Bosses who ignore and stomp on their subordinates' humanity sometimes generate quick gains. But in the long run, such shortsightedness undermines creativity, efficiency, and commitment."[20] Stewards are aware of their role in the relationship with each person on the team and their responsibility to help people realize their potential through the work they do. The bolder ones go a step further and help people realize their potential in life—personally and professionally.

THE SHAPE OF POSITIVE RELATIONSHIPS

A quality shared across the companies studied for this book is the attention to and importance placed on quality relationships. To illustrate this point, let's look to San Francisco–based 15Five, which I introduced earlier in this chapter. I smiled when I saw a tweet the company shared of the San Francisco team posing with surfboards. They spent part of the day surfing together. Sure, standing up and staying up on a board is an individual effort, but there is community building in surfing. People paddle away from the shore in groups. They encourage one another to stand up. Laughing, teasing, even consoling is part of the surfing experience. The team members were all smiles in the photo; clearly they had a great time together. Shared experiences help strengthen relationships. The dynamic between positive experiences and the influence on relationships is a focus of psychology researchers.

In Chapter 3, I discussed researcher Barbara Fredrickson's work that focuses on positivity. Her research found that positive emotions, like those the 15Five team likely experienced while surfing, position people for optimal functioning. People aren't distracted by negative emotions and interactions. Instead they can focus on doing a good job, and ultimately, the organization benefits. Fredrickson found that positive emotions also produce "optimal organizational functioning."[21]

An underlying message in Fredrickson's research is that emotions are contagious. This is what Professor of Management Sigal Barsade at The Wharton School of the University of Pennsylvania confirmed in her 2002 study on emotional contagion. Barsade confirmed that positive emotions that come from shared experiences are contagious and influence the social interactions of those who witness and participate in them.[22] This uncovers a simple yet important leadership insight: Your emotions will influence your employees and their performance. Be aware of your emotions and how they are setting the tone in your team's climate.

Spend Time in the Field

What then can you do to foster positive relationships? Certainly it begins with paying attention to how you communicate and interact with your team. We need to go deeper, however, for your relationships to be (more) positive.

On the practical side, Shannon Dugan, a manager at Luck Companies, works alongside her team. Despite the hot, muggy Virginia days, she gets out of her air-conditioned office and spends time with the workers in the rock yard. Dugan tells me that working alongside her team positively resonates with them: "Because if you're not doing that, they're looking at you like you're sitting in a glass house."

> *Two signs that you're not spending enough time with your team are staying in your office too long and canceling too many one-on-one meetings.*

If your work is more of the white-collar type, then spend time with each of your team members in their "field." Attend a meeting with them. Help them prepare for a presentation. Help them prepare for a sales call and go on the call with them. Show that you care about their success and want to stay in touch with their work reality. The intention is to understand their world, not to micromanage or instruct how to go about doing the work. Two signs that you're not spending enough time with your team are staying in your office too long and canceling too many one-on-one meetings.

Model Bidirectional Accountability

Jeremy Bowers, information technology manager at BambooHR, believes in making people feel special because they work for him. Bowers told me he is accountable to his employees.[23] This philosophy is not common with leaders. What is common is the accountability employees have to do good work. Bowers's view shifts accountability to be bidirectional.

For positive relationships to flourish, you must be accountable, too. For what, though? To start, you're accountable to do quality work so your employees don't have to clean up or fix your mistakes—at least with any regularity. You are, after all, human and prone to mistakes and failures. This is another area of accountability, safeguarding against unrealistic work arrangements that diminish employees' work-life mix.

Given the pressures of business today and the rate of change impacting business decisions, it's easy to pile on the work, keeping employees away from their families. You are accountable to help protect the work-life mix. You are also accountable for showing your people how to thrive in their work. Stewards take great pride in caring for their people and showing them how their potential can be realized. Make conversations about realizing potential regular in your coaching sessions. And yes, you need to have regular coaching sessions. It's a stewardship practice linked to helping people understand what they are capable of accomplishing.

Promote Employee Activism

A sign that you have a healthy relationship with your employees is their willingness to promote, and socially share or speak on behalf of, the organization. Employee activism is becoming a key marker of employee engagement or disengagement.

Social employee activism occurs when employees take to social media like Twitter or LinkedIn to act as brand ambassadors for their company—whether the action is coordinated or unprompted. Research designed by global public relations firm Weber Shandwick and KRC Research found that on LinkedIn, 61 percent of users who follow an organization are willing to advocate the benefits of working for the company, 33 percent of employees share information about their company without encouragement, and 50 percent post content about their company on social media. With 88 percent of employees using at least one social media site, it's the wise leader who, with good intention, coordinates with employees to be brand champions. Forty-nine percent of highly participative employee activists are engaged.[24]

These important employees are your early adopters of innovations. They can be highly influential when your relationship with them is bolstered by their beliefs that their opinions and ideas are heard, leaders are trustworthy, information flows, and there are opportunities to grow. Employee activism is built on a collaborative, mutually beneficial relationship.

> *The climate suffers when employees don't believe their leader has their back.*

Have Your People's Backs

When employees go to bat for you in their work, they expect you to have their backs when things go sideways. This can't be lip service. It needs to be experienced and believed. You will build deep, rich relationships with your people when they feel safe to advocate for and speak on behalf of the team. Without the safety, your team will resort to self-preservation. This won't help your relationship with your employees. It will create friction. Animosity and disbelief will permeate the team. Performance will suffer. Engagement will drop. Optimism will be replaced by a host of negative perspectives. The climate suffers when employees don't believe their leader has their back.

Recognize Employees

Much has been said and written about the importance of recognizing employees for their contributions. Yet repeatedly, lack of appreciation appears in lists of reasons why employees feel disengaged or leave an organization.

For many organizations, recognition programs fail to be meaningful. The problem starts with treating recognition as another program.

How you recognize your people needs to be rooted in a philosophy that is fiercely guarded and protected against programmatic mindsets that bureaucratize and marginalize human contribution as, "It's their job."

Barry-Wehmiller sees to it that recognition is done in a grand, celebratory style. Employees nominate their peers for a chance to win an opportunity to drive a sports car for a week. No trophy. No plaque. A red sports car for neighbors, friends, and family to ask, "What's with the awesome red car?" The winner of the sports car is revealed in fantastical style. A company-wide event is diligently planned and widely attended.[25] If you're going to recognize people for doing great work then turn it into a celebration. Avoid a rote, stale meeting that meekly acknowledges people. Celebrate. Have fun.

A positive relationship with your team is determined partly by your willingness to step away from the traditional perspective of leader-employee partnership. The relationship no longer needs to be confined by hierarchy, even when there is one. It may not be natural to intentionally think about the contagiousness of your emotions, but negative emotions are more contagious and have a longer-lasting effect on others than positive ones, so it is your responsibility to develop an awareness of how your emotions influence others. The partnership is defined by respect. Stewards relate to the humanity in their people and in the business to achieve remarkable results.

CHAPTER 10

Next Comes Trust:
Creating Community

*All of us are smarter than any of us. No one wants to connect
to a selfish person. And no one wants to connect
to someone who's always going to take.*

—SETH GODIN, KEYNOTE SPEECH AT SAP,

A SOFTWARE DEVELOPMENT COMPANY

THE LIMITATIONS OF COOPERATION

When you work with someone you don't care for but need to because it's beneficial to your goals, you cooperate with him. Award-winning professor of psychology at University of California Los Angeles Matthew Lieberman summed up the interaction this way: "People cooperate when they stand to benefit directly from the cooperative effort."[1] In this scenario, you are acting out of self-interest: You get something you need from the interaction. When you cooperate with someone or a group of people, it is not necessary to have a shared agenda. There is a common interest, but your cooperation could serve different needs and outcomes.

Consider this example. A politician agrees to be interviewed by a major TV network so he can express his views on a controversial tax increase. The politician gets airtime to share his political party's message. What does the network get? It gets a news story. Both parties cooperate with one another and get what they need, but don't necessarily have a shared agenda.

Cooperation isn't bad. It's incredibly useful to accomplish your goals. It's ethical and respectable when cooperative behaviors are for the mutual benefit of everyone involved. Yet for optimistic work environments, cooperation or self-interest isn't enough for success. You'll have to create a more compelling climate that fosters collaboration. Through collaborative efforts, people generate new insights not possible when working solo. People are exposed to different perspectives and can create something together impossible without collaboration. Through collaboration, resources and people are shared. The sharing of resources and people is done because what knits a strong collaborative team together are mutual aspirations and shared goals.

What can you do to boost collaboration in your team? The list below includes examples from the companies featured in this book. They serve as models for leaders who want optimism to thrive in their teams:

❏ *Send employees to learn other parts of the business.* Luck Companies has all new employees spend time at the rock quarries. Why? The quarries are the heart of the business. They're what puts food on the table, many employees told me. By learning how the rocks are mined and fed into various lines of Luck businesses, employees develop a respect for the art and science of mining rocks.

❏ *Inquire regularly into the team's effectiveness.* San Francisco–based 15Five models what it sells: engagement through communications. Every week, the software company asks its employees targeted questions to see how they are doing. Leaders and employees identify and resolve problems or celebrate successes through the transparent communications patterns. Knowing what's going on in the organization removes information barriers that often derail collaboration.

❏ *Screen for collaborative tendencies during new-hire interviews.* Menlo Innovations tests for job candidates' collaboration tendencies in a simple yet profound exercise. Candidates are put into pairs. They're given a challenge to solve and told that their goal is to make their partner look good. People with a tendency to collaborate make it to the next stage in the hiring process. In your interviews, don't ask questions about candidates' abilities to partner with others. Devise an exercise that forces them to show if they can easily partner with others to do good work. Collaboration is not merely an action, it's also a mindset.

❏ *Develop routines that reinforce collaboration.* At HopeLab, employees work together to plan celebrations. People from across the nonprofit work hard to tailor the celebration to match the occasion. The day I visited, a baby shower was planned for a team member going out on maternity leave. A special calendar with team members—male and female—who appeared to be pregnant was made for the expecting mom. The meaningful gift was met with a big smile and proud team members. The team members' ability to collaborate reinforced their deep connections with each other.

❏ *Create spaces for random collisions.* One of my favorite yearly events is Business Innovation Factory (BIF), in Providence, Rhode Island. Part of the BIF culture is RCUS: random collisions of unusual suspects. The intent behind making RCUS is to let your curiosity lead you to spontaneously meet new people, connect people and ideas, and have fun. The RCUS concept serves as a strong reminder of the importance of collaboration. What's key here, though, is that the physical workspace needs to foster such interactions. While the debate continues as to the value of open workspaces, research out of the Massachusetts Institute of Technology shows that when people randomly collide, better ideas begin to emerge. What facilitates quality collisions are three communication elements. First is energy, or the number and nature of interactions with others. Second is engagement. This focuses on the interaction patterns of people on the team. Highly engaged teams interact with one another in relatively equal amounts. Social loafing doesn't occur in these teams. Third is exploration, or communicating with others outside the team and bringing back information that is valuable to the team's work.[2] The importance of collisions has captured the attention of Zappos CEO Tony Hsieh. Zappos, the popular online shoe retailer, is experimenting with creating a coworking space in its Las Vegas headquarters that is open to the company's employees and to nonemployees from within the community. With employees and nonemployees interacting in a shared space, encouraging results emerged: Ten new community projects started, Zappos saw a 78 percent increase in submitted proposals to solve business problems, and there was an 84 percent increase in new leaders helping with project work. The early success of the experiment led to a new Zappos metric: "collisionable hours." The metric measures the number of potential collisions per hour per acre. It's a numbers game: The more collisions the higher likelihood of people finding solutions that benefit Zappos and the community.[3] The insight for stewards is to stop using meetings as an excuse for not colliding (collaborating) with others. Meet with internal and community stakeholders. Experiment with open workspace environments. Co-locate project teams to encourage collisions and collaboration. Your organization could see an increase in creative and innovative solutions.

❏ *Make time for face-to-face meetings.* It's hard to achieve and maintain quality collaborative relationships when the interactions are mostly virtual. While such interactions help organizations be flexible with remote working arrangements, they need to find a balance between working remotely and on-site. Collaborative partnerships need strong relationships. Despite geographic constraints, make time regularly to bring your team together for in-person meetings. At this time, researchers are split about the effectiveness of remote working arrangements. Still, nothing can replace the supremacy of interacting with a team that's bodily in the same room.

Cooperation and collaboration are not two sides of the same coin. The unifying influence of collaboration is strongest on the work environment. Researchers Jane Dutton of the University of Michigan and Emily Heaphy of Boston University write that "high-quality connections literally and figuratively enliven people."[4] The adept steward knows when collaboration is necessary and when a situation calls for cooperation. Your focus should be on which two will best yield mutually beneficial outcomes with maximum impact on all involved.

EQUATION FOR COMMUNITY

Collaboration is part of a critical equation important to the optimistic workplace. Not only is collaboration key, so, too, is connection among people, including the leader. When collaboration is combined with connection, a community emerges. All stewards need to remember that:

Collaboration + Connection = Community

I call this the Equation for Community. If the Origins of Optimism are the bones to creating workplace optimism, and purpose and meaningfulness are the heart, then the Equation for Community is the blood that oxygenates the entire system.

The three parts to the equation are important by themselves. When you combine them, their influence magnifies. Collaboration is the active participation of people working jointly together. Connection is a relationship between people focused on and held together by evolving shared interests. Community is a unified group of people with a shared interest. Each part of the equation feeds naturally into the other.

While too often groups of people develop a self-interest in winning and success, the Equation for Community helps people move past it. How? The very nature of each element of the equation strengthens only when the focus is on the group, or the team. As I said earlier, no one person is more important than the team. The Equation for Community reinforces achieving success for the greater good, not for the select few.

CONNECTION IS IN OUR BIOLOGY

What I hope you see is that honoring the human side of business as expressed through belonging and connectedness is not only good for people and business but also addresses the biology of human beings. Like belonging, the need for connection is a result of how our brain is wired. Neuroscience is revealing fascinating insights that can shed light on leadership activities that will foster belonging and connection. As a leader, you can intentionally create a safe, caring, and optimistic environment by knowing a little about oxytocin.

Oxytocin is a neuropeptide that the brain releases to promote social behaviors like trusting and building relationships. It's oxytocin that, in part, impels moms to care for their crying newborns and not turn away out of frustration. Oxytocin also plays a part in driving us to care for others, including strangers, who may be wounded. Time spent on social media and giving and receiving hugs have also triggered the release of this chemical.[5] In short, oxytocin helps connect us to people. The more you show that you care for people and their success, the more their brains release oxytocin and help create or deepen connections.

What then are actions you can take to deepen connections with your team? As the second part of the Equation for Community, connection is the bonding agent that links collaboration to community. Connection is more than a link. It's what enriches the collaborative experience and gives meaning to community. With that in mind, here are some ideas to help build connection.

First, always be sure your people know each other and know what everyone is working on. This builds awareness of the team's shared focus and reduces the chances of isolationism. You can accomplish this by holding daily team huddles or stand-up meetings.

Next, when you bring on new hires, pair them with someone from your team. Be sure the formal partnership lasts at least three months. This gives the two team members time to discuss the nuances of the culture and other work realities that shape how things get done on your team and in the organization. Use technology to help communicate updates that help people make sense of what's happening or that will influence their work.

At HopeLab, Chris Marcell-Murchison created the "Check-in Deck: An Invitation for Presence and Connection" to open up meetings in an intentional manner. The deck of cards features different types of activities to help people get acquainted or stay connected. Depending on what you want to accomplish, there are group activities that facilitate connection or help people be emotionally present to help the meeting be more successful. You can download the deck for free. Simply Google "Check-in Deck HopeLab" to download the PDF. It's a great tool to intentionally build workplace optimism through connection.

WHEN WE IGNORE OTHERS

Imagine you are a new team member and you walk into the lunchroom alone on your first day. The laughter and conversation are at a peak; it's shortly after 12:30 p.m., the busiest time. You find a spot at a table full of men and women talking. You sit down, open your bag lunch, and begin to unpack it, all the while overhearing several interesting conversations. You don't want to add to any of them out of concern for being rude. After all, you don't know anyone.

As you eat your lunch, no one acknowledges you, not even with a slight head nod. After lunch, you head to the conference room for your next meeting. You're early. People slowly trickle in and look at you. Some smile weakly. Promptly at the top of the hour, the meeting starts. No one officially welcomes you. Disappointed, you busy yourself taking notes but have no clue what is being discussed because the conversation is filled with corporate jargon.

New research in the organizational sciences is studying the effects of being ignored (also known as ostracism) versus being harassed to learn which of the two is more damaging to a person's psychological well-being.[6]

In the above scenario, you are ostracized. Most of us believe that harassment is more damaging than being ignored. After all, if you are verbally harassed, that, too, is damaging psychologically, right?

The findings of the research might surprise you. For starters, ostracized employees have a higher turnover rate than do those who are harassed. Researchers learned that some attention is better than none at all, even if it's negative. When a person is harassed there is at least some interaction.[7]

While relationships are damaged by harassment, there is no relationship when a person is ostracized. And this turns out to be more difficult for us to handle.

Our brains are wired to seek out groups to which we can belong. Ostracizing people prevents them from belonging. Being ignored at work is more damaging than being bullied. Ignoring people isolates them, causing pain and discomfort. It signals to people that they are not worth the effort to say hello to and that they are inconsequential. These are charged words and disturbing findings. If you've ever been shunned by a group or an individual, the memories can be painful.

> *Ostracized employees have a higher turnover rate than do those who are harassed.*

The pain of being ignored is deeply rooted in our biological need to belong. Belonging is a human motivation. When we can't form long-term, caring relationships that are reciprocal, our motivation is negatively influenced.[8]

In a work context, this leads to lower morale, higher turnover rates, and negative feelings about working for the company. This is precisely why stewards must work diligently to create an environment where people are welcomed and feel a sense of belonging through strong, mutually beneficial relationships.

Belonging is a deep sense of connectedness to a group and to select individuals. It is through connectedness that we can find meaning in our work. Connectedness makes us smarter, as we're exposed to a more diverse set of perspectives and can learn from people's experiences. Researchers have learned that relationships are key to our physical health, advancement in our thinking, and finding meaning in life.[9]

Team solidarity and positive team and self-identities are possible when people can bond. The human drive to bond is linked to positive emotions like love and caring.[10] These are two taboo topics that have historically struggled to find their place in corporate vernacular. Leaders have shied away from using these words, given the perceived awkwardness of letting their actions reflect that they care about, and even love, their people and customers. Their denial in the workplace goes against human nature and limits the depth of connectedness you can create for your team.

> *Team solidarity and positive team and self-identities are possible when people can bond.*

Human-centered businesses, like Luck Companies and Zingerman's, boldly proclaim that they have love affairs with their associates and customers. Luck Companies believes in helping its associates live fulfilling lives. It participates in this journey by finding ways to unlock its people's potential and showing them how to take care of their emotional and psychological well-being.

Zingerman's, a family of businesses in Ann Arbor, Michigan, has had a long love affair with its customers and suppliers. Zingerman's Coffee develops a close relationship with its bean growers by learning their needs as growers and what is important to their communities. In return, Zingerman's gets coffee beans that meet its quality standards and satisfy its customers. The mutually beneficial relationships help both parties do meaningful work together. The mutuality strengthens the relationship, a characteristic of belonging.

Another powerful demonstration of love and caring played out when I was visiting with Zingerman's CEO, Ari Weinzweig. We were at his coffeehouse discussing my visit when Ari got a twinkle in his eye and asked me to turn around. "Watch this," he said, of an unfolding employee-customer interaction. The employee needed to let the customer know that she was out of the tea he had requested. Rather than deliver the minimum level of customer service, the guest received a recommendation for a similar tea complete with a knowledgeable explanation of the tea's contents, origins, and flavors. "She's only 16," Ari said, his pride apparent. The customer was impressed and satisfied.

When you intentionally create connection, there's no tolerance for ostracism. The expectation and demonstration of love and caring establishes that all people will be welcomed and honored.

As a steward, you create the conditions for connectedness and model the behaviors so that it can emerge, as in the example from Zingerman's. A deeper connection with your team, customers, and even suppliers is integral to influencing the climate to be marked with optimism.

Out of this deeper connection comes a sense of greater relatedness. Employees feel understood by you. They also engage in meaningful dialogue with each other; there is no room for gossip that shreds the bonds that form. People are having fun together as demonstrated by celebrations, showing small gestures of gratitude, going out for coffee together, and even pausing during the day to chat with peers about nonwork topics.

THE TRUST GAME

There's a well-known experiment in the social sciences called the trust game. The game works like this: There are two players, and each is given $10. The game is played without the players seeing one another. Player 1 initiates the game by deciding if he will send some of his $10 to Player 2. Money decisions are entered into a computer. It's important to note that *if* Person 1 sends money to Person 2 the amount sent is automatically tripled. Person 2 then decides if she will reciprocate by giving none, all, or some of the money back to Person 1.

Person 1's first move is an act of trust. Person 1 doesn't know Person 2, so he must have some level of trust that his transfer will yield some return. If Person 2 returns some of the transferred money, this is an act of trustworthiness; after all, to be sent money by a stranger and to return some or all of it signals that Person 2 can be trusted to play the game. But why would Person 1 even send money to Person 2? Why not just walk away with $10? Why would Person 1 send money that would triple in value to someone he doesn't know, or can't see?

These are the questions scientist Paul Zak sought to answer in an experiment using the trust game. He found that 85 percent of people in the Person 1 role sent some money. Those who received the money reciprocated 98 percent of the time.

In Zak's experiments, he drew blood after each move Person 1 or 2 made. What was he testing for? Oxytocin. What he discovered was that Person 2's brain produced oxytocin when she was sent money. In fact, the more money sent, the more oxytocin the brain produced. As an act of trustworthiness, Person 2 returned more money to her trusted, anonymous partner. In an article for *Scientific American*, Zak wrote, "Receiving a signal of trust appears to make people feel positive about strangers who have trusted them."[11] Interestingly, the oxytocin levels increased only in those who were in the Person 2 role. The trustworthy response from those in the second role encouraged those in the first that their trust was not misbegotten.

In a separate experiment, Zak gave oxytocin nasal sprays to those in the first role to see how it would influence the amount they would send to Person 2. Those who initiated the transfer and had the nasal spray gave 17 percent more money to their lab partners. In some cases they sent all their money. To account for this, a conclusion Zak reaches is that oxytocin, in some patients, reduces anxiety from interacting with strangers, motivating them to send more money on the first interaction.

What's important about Zak's research is that oxytocin provides a biological explanation for connection. Outside the lab we can consciously demonstrate trust or be trustworthy. When we extend trust or act trustworthy it deepens connections with others.

The idea that trust is central to forming and deepening connections may not be a surprise. A metaphorical handshake takes place when you extend trust and the person responds in a trustworthy manner. This handshake encourages you to trust the person more, which in turn encourages more trustworthy behavior on his part. Analyzing the research, I noticed a pattern that helps complete the handshake between truster and trustworthy partner. I call this pattern the Triad of Trust.

TRIAD OF TRUST

A way to influence meaningful connections among people on your team is through the Triad of Trust. It's elements are a mindset, an emotion, and a behavior: giver's mentality, empathy, and reciprocity.

A giver's mentality takes the perspective of the other person. Rather than focusing first on what you can get or how you can benefit from a relationship, this mindset centers on how you can help the other person. You're still interested in a mutually beneficial arrangement. The nuance, however, puts the other person's needs, wants, and hopes first. A giver seeks to find ways to help people fulfill their needs, understand their wants, and realize their hopes. This is a powerful way for a steward to show trustworthiness.

> *A giver seeks to find ways to help people fulfill their needs, understand their wants, and realize their hopes.*

Empathy is understanding another person's emotions and caring enough to imagine what those emotions might be like for him. It shows a deeper commitment to not judging the person for how he might be feeling but instead showing understanding.

Finally, reciprocity is simply showing your willingness to pay forward kindness that was shown to you. In reciprocal relationships, there is no one-to-one count for paying back someone's good deed. The act of reciprocity is done merely because it was extended to you or you observed someone extend it to another. Woven together, these three elements help you deepen connections within your team and in your relationships.

Are you worth trusting as a leader? You need to be seen as trustworthy, too. In Zak's experiments, Person 1 trusted partners more when they shared some of the money they were sent. This holds a key insight for you as a steward.

In the experiment, the money is a metaphor, representing something highly valued and desirable. In the workplace, this can be success, recognition, or a high-profile project. It varies for each person you lead. Learn what is important to your staff members and then help them achieve their goals. It doesn't matter if those goals are professionally related or not. If your employees want to be promoted off your team, help them develop the skills to do so. You cannot control how long your employees stay with you. Make the most of the time you have with them. By showing that you want to help them live up to their potential, you may have them as team members longer.

Show that you are worthy of trust by providing feedback that helps employees improve. Remove barriers to progress in work. Hold regular one-on-ones with each team member. Build trust by being trustworthy. Remember Jim Kouzes and Barry Posner's DWYSYWD: Do what you say you will do. Receive trust by developing a mutually beneficial relationship with each person you lead.

As Emmy Award–winning journalist Kare Anderson advocates, find the sweet spot. This is the place where your interests and those of each person with whom you collaborate come together to create something beneficial for everyone involved.[12] Can you deepen connection without trust? Sure, but it will take an exhausting level of effort that is unsustainable, and the results will be limited.

LYIN' AND LAUGHIN'

I love the symbolism in the phrase lyin' and laughin'. Kelly Morris from Luck Companies used it to describe hanging out, connecting, and telling stories with his colleagues while at work. The lyin' part is telling stories. It's what we do when we like the people we work with. When you work with people you want to be around, conversation flows, stories unfold, and laughter punctuates the interaction. Amplify this type of interaction across a team and drop in a shared purpose—and you have a community.

Organizational community is marked by a shared sense of belonging among everyone. People willingly collaborate. The interactions are bonded by connection. It's probably no surprise that oxytocin helps strengthen the positive relations between people in a community.

The Equation for Community doesn't mean you as a steward focus directly on the outcome of community. Rather, the focus is on collaboration and connection. Collaboration and connection help bond a group of people together. If you were to focus directly on community and not the actions to help bring it about, the richness that comes from being part of one would seem forced and potentially fake. People would sense that the community is not real or suffers from something that just can't be identified. It is important to recognize the signs of community to help you monitor the health and effectiveness of your collaborative and connective stewardship actions:

❑ *People step in for each other naturally.* In a community, people step in to cover for each other when a member cannot fulfill a commitment. Community members must know each other's skill sets and be able to carry out each other's tasks.

❑ *Sacred objects unify the team.* Connected team members will naturally find through the course of time an object or objects that represent an important moment in their history. These sacred objects become part of the team's history and its culture. They are ritually shared by older team members with newer ones.

❑ *Emphasis is placed on mutually beneficial relationships.* Personal agendas don't dominate the growth of relationships. People can shift their focus to what's best for the growth of the community.

❑ *Knowledge and growth unify the community.* When people come together in a community, they learn from each other's diverse perspectives and bring about better results together.

❑ *Productive conflict is practiced.* Productive conflict is rooted in respect for the relationship and for the other person's or people's perspective. Differences within the community are brought to light and dealt with. Drama triangles are not tolerated.

❑ *Social loafing isn't tolerated.* In a healthy community, people participate to advance the cause and create results that matter to it. Social loafing is when people are allowed to ride the coattails of others. There is no room for this in healthy communities.

Consider the influence each of these elements of community has on climate. When they are viewed positively, each one, separately and combined, leaves people feeling good about their place in the community, and in the work that the community does together. Ultimately, these elements give people a sense of optimism—that good things are possible from the work the community does. It's also about the work each person contributes. We all want to believe and feel that we're part of something important.

Stewards weave together these various practices to make a place of work worth coming to each day. Your people have a choice where they work. Make that choice meaningful. Make it fulfilling. Make it count for them and for their families, too.

CHAPTER 11

The Cultivation of Optimism

The fact is, you inherited most of your management beliefs from others. . . . It's time to reexamine your heirloom beliefs.
—GARY HAMEL, *THE FUTURE OF MANAGEMENT*

THE MIGHTY START SMALL

Start small. That was one piece of common advice I received when I interviewed employees on what they would recommend to leaders who want to create workplace optimism. Forget about the "big bang" approach to shifting the climate. Don't plan a big announcement trumpeting the arrival of the next thing that will make work great. This overused management play has done nothing but tune employees' BS detector to "highly sensitive."

The other common advice was to show that you care about the conditions that shape how your team perceives the workplace. Start small and show you care. Notice what's common here? The advice is intimate. It's genuine. It's relational. The richness in the two seemingly simple pieces of advice is weighted with significance: It reflects a shift in the quality of relationship employees hope to have with you. It also sheds light on the skills you need to cocreate the optimistic workplace.

The skills required represent a subtle shift in how you show up. The shift is away from dominant management beliefs and actions to those needed of a steward who is responsible for shaping the context that helps everyone on the team do their best work. In part, the shift relies on traditional leadership skills—motivate, inspire, coach, for example. Yet the subtleties for stewardship require added finesse in not only creating an optimistic workplace but also in creating "the best outcomes, even if it's uncomfortable," says BambooHR cofounder Ryan Sanders.[1]

Thirteen years of data show that employees are not using their talents to do their best work.[2] It will take small and consistent actions from you to contribute to reversing this dismal data point. Underlying the shift to stewardship is a fundamental belief that people can be trusted and are not lazy. The belief that people want to make a difference in their world and be part of something bigger is a driver for a stewardship approach that inspires and motivates people to do their best. Money is rarely the prime motivator for employee performance. You can have a significant influence over your employees' performance if you relate to them as human beings. The skills included in this chapter will help you achieve strong relationships with your team, help you create and shape an optimistic work environment, and help you achieve desired results together. What's unique about the skills is their specificity to creating workplace optimism.

WISDOM LOOPS

The proliferation of optimistic workplaces is undoubtedly linked to the talents and willingness of leaders who supplant the beliefs of management for those of stewardship. Relying on "old tapes" of how things once were will limit your growth as a steward. Organizations will remain hindered in their adaptation to the changing realities of organizational life.

Wisdom loops will help you remain relevant. There are three elements to them, starting with your unlimited potential. As you explore your potential—or your employees'—you learn (the second element) more about yourself and your craft. This helps you grow (the third element) as a human being and leader and expands your body of work.

As you grow, you expand your potential, starting an upward spiral that elevates your potential. The wisdom loop repeats itself. The rhythm of the loops goes like this: Your potential helps you learn, which in turn helps you grow, which in turn unleashes more of your potential. By developing any of the skills and traits listed below, you enter into a wisdom loop.

PORTRAIT OF A STEWARD

Skills and traits categorically linked to strategic thinking, global thinking, and design thinking are important for a well-rounded steward. Those, however, are not the focus here. The skills and traits included in this chapter fall under two categories: Self and Us. Those listed under the Self category are the highest-value skills or traits that are needed to bring optimism to the forefront of people's experience at work. Those in the Us category rely on skills or traits necessary to deepen connection among members of your team as well as to create a sense of belonging that people experience while working in your team.

Some of the items below may be familiar, while a few may be new to you. The contents of the lists come from a variety of sources. I reflected back on my 20-plus years as an organizational change management practitioner and looked for themes that surfaced for leaders who were willing to create a great work environment. I then closely examined the interview transcripts for this book for themes about skills necessary to create the optimistic workplace. Also, I examined how change triggers influence the way organizations operate now and in the future. Over time, the things employees want from their employers have changed; technology is shifting how and where we work, shaping the nature and quality of our interactions.

Finally, great thinkers of our time like Angela Duckworth and Martin Seligman influenced my thinking about what it takes for stewards to be effective in their role as optimism makers. I synthesized these varying elements to create the portrait of a steward captured below. They reflect a mixture of experience and input from people in the trenches and academics doing quality research that help us relate better to and understand people.

I purposely avoided identifying strengths. Strengths are different from skills. Skills reflect competence. The philosophy of strengths contends that when we focus on our talents, our growth is greatest, as opposed to the limited growth that comes from a focus on weaknesses.

Donald Clifton, considered to be the father of strengths-based psychology, explains, "A strength is mastery created when one's most powerful talents are refined with practice and combined with acquired relevant skills and knowledge."[3] Also, strengths are energizers. For example, I have the strength of creativity. When I can be creative in my work, I'm energized. Strengths, however, are not necessarily a reflection of skill. I may be energized by design work, but I am not skilled at creating vector images important for the design project to be successful. Strengths are not listed here because I believe there exist other resources that can help you determine what your strengths are, Strengthscope assessment, for example.[4]

You cannot work on all the skills below at once. Skills take time to develop and improve. You should be able to identify which skills and/or traits you should focus on given your current circumstances. When I coach other leaders, we select no more than two to three skills to focus on. That helps reduce the anxiety and frustration inherent in personal development and growth. Spreading your attention across too many areas also limits your potential.

Know Yourself

Socrates set the bar high when he said, "The unexamined life is not worth living." Your biases about the "right" way to live and your perceptions about people make you believe you are an authority on both; you don't argue with your own conclusions. You assume what you think and see is right. Self skills and traits provide needed balance against your biases. Their purpose is to position you to be more curious about what happens around you, to be inquisitive rather than to routinely believe your initial conclusions are always accurate.

> *Relating to human beings is troubling when you choose to not become more self-aware.*

Self skills position you to balance gut and experience with data and evidence. To rely solely on one grouping over the other hampers your ability to make sense of what is going on around you and internally. Without an evolving sense of awareness of who you are and an active inquiry into why you believe what you do, you risk reducing your leadership effectiveness. Relating to human beings is troubling when you choose to not become more self-aware. Your ability to shape an energizing environment is crippled. To create workplace optimism you must know how to assess the way your presence influences your team, both positively and negatively.

It's important to recognize that you already are talented in many of the skill areas. Likewise, you probably have some of the traits listed below. It is not egotistical to believe that you demonstrate or possess any of them. Give yourself credit for what you do well and who you already are. The confidence will help you build stronger relationships.

❑ *Humility.* It's fitting to list first the trait of humility. The success and joy you experience watching people flourish and live up to their potential can be deeply gratifying. It can stroke the ego. Humility helps keep you grounded. It helps you build stronger relationships, a key factor in fashioning the optimistic workplace. It's also a key ingredient to seeing your flaws and strengths and appreciating them in others. The pursuit of success, while important to your own aspirations, is also done for the greater good. Research shows that the humble CEO gains acceptance from her team and those in the middle layers when she appeals to shared interests and downplays a dominating influence of ego.[5] If this is true at the upper levels of an organization, imagine the powerful influence a humble manager has on the team. Keep in mind that employees' immediate managers have a greater influence on their perceptions and work experiences than do CEOs. Humble stewards establish an expectation of behavioral norms that are key to creating an energizing and empowering climate, for example, inclusive decision making, sharing power to help others be successful, even expressing and showing that the leader needs others.[6]

❑ *Honesty.* There are two dimensions to honesty: being honest with yourself and with others. Self-honesty helps you assess situations and your response to them realistically. This can be done with positive or uncomfortable realities. Take, for example, a situation in which your team landed a major client for the firm. You helped coach the team on effective relationship-building approaches that contributed to landing the new contract. A person being honest with himself would take some credit for the win. Certainly a principled steward would also admit some fault if he hadn't provided the needed coaching to support the team's efforts. The other side of honesty is how you express your thoughts and feelings to others. Do you show a sincere side of your personality that builds and deepens relationships? Are you respectful but honest when sharing difficult feedback? An honest steward builds trust and credibility. Others can predict with some accuracy what you might do and say. Trust, credibility, and predictability are outcomes you want to create by being honest. Using honesty to damage relationships and partnerships has no place in the optimistic workplace.

❏ *Reflection.* This can be my personal Achilles' heel. When I'm on autopilot, I can easily overlook the need to reflect on what's happening around me. I've learned after several difficult situations that it's important to find the pause button, step away from my first reaction, and quiet my mind. Take time to reflect so you can connect the dots between people and events to make sense of what's happening around you. You don't want to overlook patterns that can interfere with your work to create optimism. The same can be said about seeing patterns that will enable you to create the type of environment that helps others be productive and even find meaning. In his message for World Communications Day 2012, Pope Benedict XVI eloquently said this about the importance of reflection in helping determine what is significant: "Silence is an integral element of communication; in its absence, words rich in content cannot exist. In silence, we are better able to listen to understand ourselves; ideas come to birth and acquire depth; we understand with greater clarity what it is we want to say and what we expect from others; and we choose how to express ourselves."[7] As a meaning maker, you possess great power to help others find fulfillment in their work. This great responsibility is better fulfilled when you routinely make time to silently think through the events that played out in the previous days, weeks, and months. Reflection helps you identify the narrative in your interactions. You are better able to establish meaningful goals and priorities. You develop focus in a noisy world.

❏ *Grit.* Participants in the Scripps National Spelling Bee reveal insights in this trait. Researcher Angela Duckworth, who studied spelling bee participants, defines grit as "perseverance and passion for long-term goals." Students who went farther in the spelling bee practiced more and were grittier than students who didn't spend as much time practicing. Duckworth's initial conclusion is common sense: Invest more time and you will do better than those who don't practice.[8] Upon deeper review, however, she found that happiness also plays an important role in a person's grit. Duckworth and her research colleagues discovered that grittier people pursue deeper levels of happiness, like engagement and meaning. The fortitude to withstand difficult circumstances and the passion to overcome them to achieve goals requires a deep commitment to do the work. This is what Duckworth refers to as engagement. And rather than chase after pleasures to find happiness, gritty people seek meaning, or to be of service to others, to experience a more fulfilling type of happiness.[9] Undoubtedly you will face challenges in cultivating optimism at work. You'll set goals, miss the mark, and recover by reflecting on what went wrong. Grit can help you endure the hardships and find greater enrichment in living while pursuing meaningful personal and professional goals.

❏ *Resilience.* The ability to recover from, adapt to, and grow from setbacks is resilience. Positive emotions like joy, interest, and pride help build resilience. Resilience helps generate positive emotions.[10] Is resilience something you just have, or can you grow to be more resilient? The good news is, the answer is yes to the latter. You build resilience throughout your life. Positive emotions help you strengthen your ability to learn from life's troubles. The dual relationship between resilience and positive emotions helps increase your life satisfaction.[11] So what's important about resilience in relation to optimism? Frankly, your efforts will likely meet some level of resistance from skeptical employees. Your peers may think it's not possible for your workplace. Resilience is necessary to help you persevere through the doubt and frustrations. Positive emotions will help see you through the difficult times. Now, these statements are based on the assumption that workplace optimism is not part of climate. For those who have some level of optimism in the workplace, resilience and positive emotions are key to help you overcome challenges that threaten to minimize the positive vibe that you and your team have created. This trait is a remarkable source of happiness that can lead you to great achievements that can make a difference for you and those you lead.

❏ *Sense Making.* A skill related to reflection, sense making is your ability to inquire into, not judge, a situation to learn its meaning.[12] For example, you learn that your team has doubts about your efforts to improve the work environment. One of your employees confides in you that several others felt your speech about needing to find purpose in work and believing that good things should come from it was just talk. Most didn't believe that you'd really follow through. Even a few view work solely as something necessary to put food on the table; they don't need meaning and purpose in their work. Rather than react to the feedback, you decide to observe the team's actions and learn the meaning behind their doubt. You avoid blaming and labeling your employees. (The very act of labeling limits your scope of sense making. Labeling the team as lazy or closed-minded only puts up barriers to understanding. The labels are judgments and personal. Both will prevent a richer relationship from forming.) Learning the meaning behind their doubt better positions you to connect with your team members and help them overcome what is causing the suspicion of your intent. Your approach to observe helps you learn what is important and what is merely noise. Ultimately, sense making is about understanding so you can take action to respond in the best manner possible to a situation or circumstance. In the above scenario, a strong way to respond would be to meet individually with team members and inquire into their thinking. Test your conclusions against what you learn from the conversations. Adapt your conclusions as you gain more information, remaining open to realities you hadn't considered. Different perspectives are invaluable to sense making. By showing your interest in learning the meaning behind people's words and actions, you create a path for mutual understanding and greater chances for collaboration. This is invaluable for cultivating optimism.

❑ *Vulnerability.* In the machinations of business, many of us have gained the ability to present a strong demeanor. Don't let people see you upset. Maintain a facade of strength; don't let people see your weaknesses. This is outdated chicanery and certainly will not help bring about the optimistic workplace. A human-centered workplace makes room for vulnerability. We can relate more deeply to people when we know they also have struggles. We all experience it. Many deny its influence on our thoughts and actions. But vulnerability cannot be quieted. It's most influential when we accept its presence. It's destructive when we deny its gut-wrenching existence. Vulnerability is not weakness. It takes strength to show it. Despite feeling vulnerable, you show up. We all must be willing to show vulnerability if we are to have meaningful relationships with others. Showing vulnerability is essential to exploring purpose. It's essential to making decisions that may not be what you want but what's needed. It may involve sharing information that does not represent your best side. Conversely, it may involve sharing something that is great but that you worry about being judged as "better than." Showing vulnerability takes grit and courage. The skill is in silencing the committee in your head that says play it safe, don't reveal your hand. The beauty of showing vulnerability is that it allows people to get closer to you. This helps you be a more relatable and perhaps stronger leader than the one hiding behind a facade of strength.

For the Greater Good

Where Self skills and traits focus on raising awareness of who you are so you can have greater impact on people and results, Us skills and traits aim to make life better for human beings. Those listed below help you unleash people's potential. They support your work as a steward in helping people uncover and live up to their purpose and discover meaning in their work. I'm including some that are less obvious. Notably excluded from the list are coaching and mentoring. These skills are vital to helping people grow, but I've not listed them because they are more obvious. Also not included are skills that have been thoroughly examined throughout the book, for example, collaboration and making meaning. One final point: You can't create an optimistic workplace by yourself. It's a community effort. The skills below reinforce this philosophy. Creating change can't be done in a vacuum or in secrecy.

❑ *Noticing.* BambooHR cofounder Ryan Sanders explains this skill as paying attention to the overt and subtle ways people positively contribute to the team and its goals.[13] The skill of noticing is nuanced and unique to each leader. For Sanders, noticing includes sending a thank-you email to a group of new employees doing great in training. This noticing act carries profound significance when it comes from a founder. For Sanders's business partner, Ben Peterson, noticing included customizing a sincere thank-you for a sales employee who hit a milestone in his goals. This employee loves shoes. Knowing this, Peterson bought him two pairs of basketball shoes to add to his collection.[14] Sanders and Peterson take time to notice what's important to people. Underneath the act of noticing is a genuine curiosity about people and learning what's important to them. Noticing also is helpful during difficult discussions. Dan Cawley, chief operating officer at HopeLab, uses noticing as a way to help people live more fully into their potential. In interviews with me, Cawley and those who work closely with him gave numerous examples of his asking inquisitive questions when he notices another person's discomfort.[15] There are four key behaviors linked to the noticing skill: asking open-ended questions; recognition, for example for accomplishments or milestones; showing appreciation; and having compassion for people's well-being and happiness. It's a selfless skill. The four behaviors help express how you care for others.

❑ *Connecting.* Business has been and always will be built on the backs of relationships. Thankfully, human beings are still essential to doing a majority of the work needed in organizations. As I've said previously, the one relationship that has been largely ignored is the one between employee and employer. The employer is mostly represented by the employee's immediate boss. It's been a contentious relationship that no longer fits today's realities. The demands on people are greater as competition and the rate of change keeps organizations on their toes. What is needed today is a relationship innovation. Your relationship with employees needs to go from transactional to relational. A skill critical to such innovation involves connecting your people to the resources they need to reach their potential. You are an advocate for their growth. If your employees need access to people, go to bat for them. If they need resources like money or time and the business case is strong, advocate for the resources. The days when employees' ideas and requests died with the manager and went unheard ended when human potential became a paramount concern for stewards.

❑ *Experimenting.* Menlo Innovations CEO Rich Sheridan likes to say, "Let's run an experiment."[16] It was his willingness to try new ideas that might make his business a better place to work that led to allowing newborn babies in the workplace. Or consider Zingerman's approach to expanding into new business areas. When approved by the company's partners, the associate who thinks of a new business is given some money to see if she can make the business grow. These are examples of big experiments and may not reflect what you may do. They hold insights that are key to the skill of experimenting. First, shape the conditions in your team that signal to employees it's all right to experiment. Leaders at Menlo Innovations and Zingerman's make failure acceptable by encouraging people to take risks in how they approach their work and to learn quickly from mistakes. Show your team how you are experimenting. Openly share what's working and not working. BambooHR uses what it calls an Oops Email that goes out when people make a mistake that has a serious impact on others in the organization. There is no policy about when to send such an email or what to include in it. It's intended to remove the shame and embarrassment of making mistakes. The premise is simple: Explain what went wrong and how it will be fixed.[17] If people are allowed to hide behind mistakes, it reduces the likelihood of people experimenting to make the organization stronger. You'll rely on experimenting when you work with your team to give shape to a strong optimistic culture. You'll run experiments with your team to see what works and what doesn't help people have a shared, positive experience at work.

❏ *Prioritizing.* At first glance, this skill may seem unrelated. But it is the most crucial in creating workplace optimism. Competing demands and priorities threaten to erode whatever goodwill exists and to cripple the positive environment. Against a backdrop of too much work and not enough resources, you cannot afford to have employees unclear about what work is important, why it's a priority, and how it creates value for the team and organization. Your ability to prioritize with each of your employees their workload positions them to make progress on what matters. A lack of progress in work will also erode and cripple the effects of workplace optimism.

How do you determine which skills to develop or traits to strengthen? That depends. You need clarity on what optimism looks like in your environment. If the quality of the work experience is not where you need it to be, then select two to three skills and/or traits that will help you get closer to what you want. If you're unsure of what the environment is altogether, then select items from the list that will help you get the clarity you need. I also suggest that you spend time going through the Optimism Planner in Appendix 1. It will guide you through a process to help you map out what needs to be done to create an optimistic workplace.

What Self and Us skills and traits have in common is their humanity. They help you become more relatable and more understanding of your employees' aspirations. Cultivating workplace optimism is something you'll go through together with your team.

The journey to optimism can only be a shared one. A great deal of self-development comes with the work. If there's any message I hope you get from reading this book it is that we are stronger when we work together. There is no room for people who want to go it alone in the type of workplace explained here. There is, however, plenty of autonomy in how people approach their work.

The optimistic workplace is not for everyone. It's only for those who want meaning, purpose, and growth in their work. Certainly, some employees only want to show up, do what's expected, and leave. These are transactional arrangements. Managers allow this to happen. Enlightened stewards see the change in workforce expectations and are pivoting away from this outdated approach. The optimistic workplace is for those who want fulfillment in their work and in their lives. There's room for anyone who has some level of awareness of this, no matter the type of work, organizational size, or industry.

OUT FROM THE UNDERGROUND

It's ironic that the first chapter of a book about optimism starts in an underground space like Menlo Innovations. But there is no storyline of shunned, awkward misfits hoping to find their place in the world. Instead, a thriving workplace built on optimism and joy emerges.

Joy and optimism are brother and sister. They delight people and unite them under hope. Both show our resilience and belief that how things are today can be better. Like hope, optimism is rooted in our survival.

In a company report, employees of 15Five reflected on the role of optimism in the workplace. Their thoughtfulness ranges from doing the "greatest good" to getting "caught up in [a] wave of optimism" to triumphing over the status quo.[18] The tug of workplace optimism on people's perceptions can transform how one might naturally feel and see the workplace in new, inspiring ways.

Optimism reveals our humanity. In times of anguish, optimism emerges as a path forward. When we are happy, it elevates us even higher. The versatility of optimism builds possibility. It catapults us from the shackles of a dreary state.

Optimism's power also unfolds in our workplaces. In a time where employees can hardly stand or trust their leaders, or struggle to find joy in their commitment to their work, the optimistic workplace shines brightly on a new path forward. It brings hope and humanity to work. It's a pivot away from the oppressive traditions of 19th- and 20th-century beliefs about work's role in our lives.

People on your team are hungry for their work to be a positive influence in their lives. You have an amazing opportunity to give this to them. No permission slip is needed from the higher-ups in your organization. You can act today. You can unite the human desire to be part of something bigger than ourselves with your company's aspirations. The combination reveals extraordinary possibilities that benefit employees, the organization, and those whom you serve.

The optimistic workplace—whether it be underground, at a coworking space, in a not-for-profit, a high-rise, or even a start-up—is a reflection of human possibility and good business. It's a mutually satisfying pairing of the two whose time has come. You only need to decide to take the first step.

Two Paths

The work of a steward is a choice. It's fulfilling work, and it's hard. It calls for leadership actions that are not commonly practiced in today's business environment. Sure, much of what is covered in this book is happening in organizations around the world. But we have a long way to go before a tipping point is reached. So creating optimism in the workplace comes down to what you do. Notable business thinker and author Jim Collins once said, "The difference is between those who could and those who did—this is a defining moment."[1]

The thing about defining moments is they can happen at any time. You simply need to commit to being in action in the service of others to be part of one. We are at a time in business when two paths have presented themselves.

One path is business as usual: It's management. It's control. Its philosophy is fear of change; keep things the way they are. As my friend and colleague Lee Scott teaches students, the familiar path is about keeping reality stable and predictable, with little variation on how things are done.[2]

The other path is business transformed: It's human centered and values based. Unpredictability is embraced as an opportunity to maximize success even when its definition is unclear or unknown. This path may appear riskier given its nature, but it's the best path forward if you want to thrive in our hyperconnected, socially enabled, relationship-centric business world. But don't worry; this path is populated with others who see the connectedness between people as a competitive advantage and not a distraction.

So in what condition do you want to leave your team? Your organization? It's a challenging question that only the bravest stewards raise their hands to answer. Step forward to do something about the dismal realities shaping your team's work experience.

The work of a steward is not about recognition. It's about improving human beings' lives so they can contribute their best in all arenas of life.

Two paths will always be available to you. I hope you choose the one that helps people use their potential for good.

The Optimism Planner

THE FIRST 30 DAYS—PLANNING

WEEK 1

1. If you didn't already do the exercise in Chapter 5, identify your top five personal values.

Accountability	Accuracy	Achievement	Aesthetics	Appreciation
Challenge	Collaboration	Community	Competence	Creativity
Curiosity	Decisiveness	Effectiveness	Excellence	Fairness
Freedom	Fun	Generosity	Growth	Hard Work
Harmony	Health	Integrity	Joy	Justice
Learning	Loyalty	Privacy	Prosperity	Relationships
Resourcefulness	Responsibility	Results	Serenity	Stability

2. Now define your top five values below.

_____

_____

_____

_____

_____

3. Where are your personal values present in your current work?

_____

_____

_____

_____

_____

4. Where in your work are your personal values absent?

_____

_____

_____

_____

_____

5. What do you notice about your values alignment or misalignment? What do you need to do to create better alignment given these insights?

_____

_____

_____

_____

_____

WEEK 2

1. What will you gain from creating a more optimistic workplace?

_____

_____

_____

_____

_____

2. What will your team gain from a more optimistic workplace?

_____

_____

_____

_____

_____

3. Given the benefits identified in the previous two questions, why do you want to create a more optimistic work climate?

_____

_____

_____

_____

_____

4. Envision the end of this work. What will be different because you did this work to create an optimistic work environment?

_____

_____

_____

_____

_____

WEEK 3

When creating change, too often we focus attention on those who we think will resist. This is a change trap. Instead you want to focus on the early adopters and the innovators—people who like new ideas and are willing to show support for them. These two groups of people are your allies. You want to know who your allies are so you can leverage their support in cultivating workplace optimism.

1. Think about who's on your team. Who would be your allies, that is, the early adopters and innovators who like new ideas and are willing to show support for them? List your allies here.

_____

_____

_____

_____

_____

2. You'll want to meet with allies to enlist their support. Here's a meeting framework:

Meeting Focus	Objective	Outcome
Reason for the meeting.	Establish a sense of urgency and enlist support for doing something about it.	Agreement that something needs to change if the workplace is going to get better.
Explain workplace optimism.	Show what you want to do to counter the current mood of the team's work environment.	Understanding of what workplace optimism is.
Enlist support.	Ask ally to support your effort when you announce the effort in an upcoming meeting.	Agreement on what support looks like.

3. Imagine you're sitting down with your team, and you're about to explain why it's important to create workplace optimism. Using your answers to the previous week's questions, write out what you'd say to your team. Remember to use benefit language that suits your team members. They'll want to know what's in it for them.

_____

_____

_____

_____

_____

4. What resistance might you encounter when you announce your intentions? Some possibilities are disbelief, indifference, desire for proof that things need to be better, anger.

_____

_____

_____

_____

_____

5. How might you overcome the resistance? Write out a response to each of the main areas where you anticipate some level of resistance.

_____

_____

_____

_____

_____

WEEK 4

It's almost time to meet with your team to discuss the work environment. Be sure to choose a date when most everyone can be present. Here's a meeting framework:

Meeting Focus	Objective	Outcome
Reason for the Meeting (5 minutes)	Establish a sense of urgency and enlist support for doing something about it. Use benefit language from Week 2 prompts 1–3.	Agreement that something needs to change if the workplace is going to get better
Current Reality (approx. 25 minutes)	Have your team members identify words that describe the good things and the effects the workplace environment has on them. Have your team members identify words that describe the effects of a negative workplace environment. (*Note:* You may need to change the word *negative* to suit your situation.)	A shared group picture of what's working and not working in the current environment
A Desired Future (approx. 30 minutes)	Introduce workplace optimism. Have your team members identify words that describe how they'd like the workplace environment to feel. Have your team members identify the effects on them if the environment felt optimistic.	A shared look forward to an environment that suits your team members and their needs to create value for the organization and for themselves
Our Next Steps (approx. 20 minutes)	Identify what the team members think should be done to take steps to bring the desired future into reality.	Agreement on next steps and support for the desired future

THE NEXT 30 DAYS— IMPLEMENTATION

WEEK 5

It's time to hold the meeting using the agenda from Week 4. You're looking to engage and build a shared understanding of the work climate.

For the "Current Reality" agenda item, do the following:

❋ Hand out a pad of 3-by-5-inch sticky notes and a marker to each person on the team.

❋ Instruct each person to come up with one to three words that describe positive aspects of the workplace and the effect the workplace environment has on them. One word per note.

❋ Have each person place the words on a prepared flip-chart sheet labeled "Current Reality."

❋ Have someone group the words into similar categories.

❋ Review the words by having each person explain her choices.

Repeat the above steps for the effects of a negative workplace environment.

Next it's time to work on "A Desired Future."

Before you hand out the notes to your team, spend some time describing the elements of an optimistic work environment. This is where you'll want to explain the Origins of Optimism: purpose, meaningful work, and community. Here are some potential points to weave into your narrative:

1. Purpose is not just about our team's purpose or the organization's. It's also about your personal purpose—what's important to you.

2. Purpose is about finding meaning from your life's experiences. It gives shape to goals you set for yourself, personally and professionally.

3. I want to help you better align with your purpose.

4. Meaningful work means finding significance in the work you're doing. It's different from purpose in that meaningful work is characterized by your understanding of how your work supports the bigger picture. You also find personal value in doing the work.

5. Community is how we support one another in our efforts to do great work. It's also learning about each other in ways that go beyond the transaction of doing work. We help each other find work-life integration. I'm committed to help you find a greater mix between the time you spend here at work and the time you need outside work.

6. Combined, the three elements of the Origins of Optimism help shape the way it feels to work here.

Next:

✳ Hand out a pad of 3-by-5-inch sticky notes and a marker to each person on the team.

✳ Instruct each person to come up with one to three words that describe how they'd like the workplace to feel. One word per note.

✳ Have each person place the words on a prepared flip-chart sheet labeled "Desired Future."

✳ Have someone group the words into similar categories.

✳ Review the words by having each person explain his choices.

Now it's time to work on "Our Next Steps."

✳ Give everyone a blank 8.5-by-11-inch sheet of paper. Have them quietly brainstorm alone what next steps they'd like to see happen to bring the desired future into reality. (*Note:* More extroverted groups will benefit from brainstorming as a large group out loud.)

✳ After they have brainstormed, go around the room and have them say what next steps they'd like to see happen.

✳ Collect the sheets from everyone. Explain that you'll type up their ideas and send the document to them. The idea is to let the ideas sit for a day in the back of their minds. New ideas, or ideas that make the ones shared stronger, may surface.

WEEK 6

1. Create a rollout plan with the ideas gathered from your team to shift the workplace climate. You'll want to add some of your ideas to the plan.

2. Question 4 from Week 2 asked you what would be different by taking on this work. Does your plan get you closer to the picture you described in Question 4? How so?

_____

_____

_____

_____

_____

3. Do you see more of your personal values coming through the plan? If not, why not? If yes, how so? Don't discount this question. Values alignment is key to your finding lasting value in this work.

_____

_____

_____

_____

_____

4. Introduce the plan in a separate meeting with your team.

WEEK 7

1. Create an Optimism Scorecard that identifies metrics that will help you visibly track your progress toward creating the optimistic workplace. Here are some examples:

Measurement: Deepen Team Trust

Metric: Percentage of team members who believe communication currently goes two ways

Measurement: Create Meaningful Work

Metric: Percentage of team members who understand how their work ties to the organization's big picture

Metric: Percentage of team members who believe their work is valued by the organization.

Measurement: Model Work-Life Integration

Metric: Percentage of team members who are pursuing personal interests outside the organization

Metric: Decrease in the amount of overtime across the team

Two things to remember:

* Don't skip this step. You'll need proof that you mean business. The scorecard is a way to hold you and your team accountable for the results.

* Make the scorecard public to the team. Creating an optimistic climate is a team endeavor. Don't try to monitor this in secret.

2. Share the plan and the scorecard with your immediate manager. Show her that you mean business and that you'll keep her informed as things progress. Keep in mind that you've not measured anything yet. That will begin in Week 9.

WEEK 8

1. Plan to have ongoing discussions about the team's progress to create a more optimistic environment in your one-on-ones. Also, make the shift personal for your employees. Here are some topics to discuss in your one-on-ones to tailor the journey to each employee:

Life aspirations	**Personal interests/ hobbies**	**Promotional/ development goals**
Life goals	**What meaningful work looks like**	**General management feedback**

THE FINAL 30 DAYS— MONITORING

WEEK 9

1. Hold an Optimism Retrospective. This is a team meeting to capture how things are going on the journey to optimism. Here's how to facilitate the retrospective:

✳ Give everyone a sticky note and a marker.

✳ Have the team draw a picture of the weather forecast for itself. The weather is a metaphor for how each person feels the team's progress is going toward creating the optimistic workplace. For example, one person might draw sunshine, another clouds and lightning.

✳ Have them place their weather forecasts on a flip-chart sheet labeled "Team Weather Forecast."

✳ Group the sticky notes into categories.

✳ Have each person explain his weather forecast. Keep in mind that this needs to be a safe environment. No one can argue or debate another person's forecast. This is a reflection of each person's experience, and everyone needs to respect that. This creates the space for people to really share what they think—good or bad.

* On a new flip-chart sheet, create two columns: "Keep Doing" and "Better Next Time."

* Have the team members brainstorm what they need to keep doing and what needs to change in order for the weather forecasts to improve. Again, no judging of ideas.

* Confirm that the "Keep Doing" column contains actions and ideas that the team can support.

* Using color dot stickers, have the team vote for the items in "Better Next Time." The items with the most votes will be the team's focus for improvement during the next 30 days.

You'll repeat the Optimism Retrospective throughout the initial stages of your work. It's up to you how long to do them. I recommend doing them for at least six months. It's another way to build account-ability and bring the team closer together. Whatever is said in the retrospective is confidential. The team needs to believe this. Once the team believes in the process and begins to see progress, the dynamics of the team improve. You're creating a space for optimism to emerge.

2. Create and send out a short survey to measure progress toward creating optimism. Create questions that align with the measures and metrics you identified in Week 7.

WEEK 10

1. Evaluate the survey results and document the themes and your recommendations for improvement. Go over these in a team meeting.

2. In the team meeting, solicit input on additional recommendations. Remember, you want shared ownership of the process. You'll reinforce this by asking for input on recommendations. I encourage you to do the same for the themes.

You may be tempted to spend hours on the survey results. Don't. You're not striving for perfection here but for some analysis to spark a conversation with your team.

WEEK 11

1. Share the survey results with your next-level manager.

2. How are you feeling about the journey to workplace optimism?

What I Like About the Journey	What Concerns Me About the Journey
_____	_____
_____	_____
_____	_____
_____	_____
_____	_____

3. What do you need to do to address your concerns?

_____

_____

_____

_____

_____

4. Are you seeing your values come through more in your work since you've started the journey to workplace optimism? If no, why not? If yes, how so?

_____

_____

_____

_____

_____

WEEK 12

When you started the work to create workplace optimism, you relied on your passion, strengths, and talents. Creating workplace optimism, however, calls on some different stewardship skills. It's time to take an inventory to see how you're doing. Below is the list of skills introduced in Chapter 11. The goal is to not be proficient in all the skills; that's just not humanly possible. The goal is to identify those skills that are key to your success and your team's success. In short, it's what matters now.

Skill	Almost Always	Often	Occasionally	Rarely
Humility				
Honesty				
Reflection				
Grit				
Resilience				
Sense making				
Vulnerability				
Noticing				
Connecting				
Experimenting				
Prioritizing				

1. What skills are helping you succeed right now with creating workplace optimism?

_____

_____

_____

_____

_____

2. What skills will you need to keep the good work going?

_____

_____

_____

_____

3. What would your team say you need to focus on?

_____

_____

_____

_____

Though these 30/60/90-day plans have an end, you'll likely find the need to repeat some of the exercises or revisit some of the questions. That's normal.

Keep your eye on your goal for doing this work. I admire you for doing it. Please reach out and let me know how things are going. You can let me know on Twitter. I'm @TheShawnMurphy. You can also email me at shawn@switchandshift.com. Also, visit the website for this book, theoptimisticworkplace.com, for more tools.

Thank you for believing that work can be a great contribution to people's lives.

One-on-One Format

Cultivate optimism by having regular one-on-one meetings with your employees. This format has four focus areas:

1. Career focus

2. Work progress focus

3. Purpose focus

4. Values-alignment focus

Career Focus

Spend time inquiring into each employee's career and professional development goals. Your objective is to help her have a thriving career.

* Learn what her career advancement desires are.

* Learn what her professional development goals are.

* Help her sync her professional development goals to her career advancement goals.

* Help her identify mentors. Ideally, they would be older than her, younger than her, and her age. This helps give a balanced perspective on career and work realities.

At least quarterly, review your employee's plans to achieve her career and professional development goals.

Work Progress Focus

This is perhaps one of the most important conversations you can have with your employees. It is human nature to want to see progress in the things we're working on. It's demotivating to not make progress in work. Your objectives in this focus area are to:

* Understand what your employee is focusing on.

* Help prioritize workload to maximize efficiencies and allow the employee to see progress.

* Identify impediments that are interfering with work progress.

* Develop a plan to remove impediments.

* Inquire into how you can better support your employee.

* Assign work that aligns with your employee's strengths—work that energizes.

* Celebrate accomplishments.

At least monthly, discuss these points.

Purpose Focus

Spend time helping your employees discover their purpose. Your objective with this conversation is to help your employees have a more fulfilling work-life mix.

* Inquire into how work is influencing your employee's personal life.

* Codevelop plans to help the employee have a more integrated work-life mix.

✳   Inquire into passion areas that may be linked to your employee's purpose.

✳   Develop plans to help your employee do more of what ignites his passions.

At least four times a year have purpose-centered conversations with your employees.

Values-Alignment Focus

Your employees need to know what they stand for. Help them more strongly integrate their values into their whole lives.

✳   Inquire into how strongly personal values are present in your employee's work.

✳   Codevelop a plan to help the employee have stronger alignment with her values and those of the organization.

✳   Give assignments that align with your employee's values whenever possible.

At least four times a year have values-alignment conversations with your employees.

Endnotes

INTRODUCTION

1. Studs Terkel, *Working: People Talk About What They Do All Day and How They Feel About What They Do* (New York: The New Press, 1972), xi.

2. Ibid.

3. Gary Hamel, *What Matters Now: How to Win in a World of Relentless Change, Ferocious Competition, and Unstoppable Innovation* (San Francisco: Jossey-Bass, 2012), 3–4.

4. Author interview with Larry Robillard, October 2014.

5. Peter Block, *Stewardship: Choosing Service over Self-Interest* (San Francisco: Berrett-Koehler), 21. Block's book is essential reading for anyone interested in looking with a fresh perspective at how we work.

CHAPTER 1: THE FUTURE OF THE WORKPLACE

1. Author interview with Rich Sheridan (CEO of Menlo Innovations), summer 2014.

2. Robert Stringer, *Leadership and Organizational Climate* (New York: Prentice Hall, 2002), 5. Stringer and his research partner, George Litwin, list six dimensions of climate: structure, standards, responsibility, recognition, support, and commitment. Building on Stringer and Litwin's research, Hay Group, a global HR consultancy and research group, lists clarity, standards, responsibility, flexibility, rewards, and team commitment as impacts to team performance. Hay Group, "Creating the Climate to Get the Most from Your Team," accessed August 30, 2014, http://www.thecqi.org/Documents/com munity/WQD/Sellafield%20presentations%202011/Sharon%20Crabtree-Mike%20Dodds.pdf.

3. Hay Group, "Leadership Effectiveness Audit," accessed August 30, 2014, http://www.haygroup.com/leadershipandtalentondemand/leadershipsolu tions/assessment-programs/leadership-effectiveness-audit.aspx?show= y?show=n.

4. Hay Group, "Improve Leadership Skills and Team Climate," accessed September 1, 2014, http://atrium.haygroup.com/ww/our-products/leadership-ben efits.aspx.

5. Stringer, *Leadership and Organizational Climate*, 10–11.

6. LinkedIn Talent Solutions, "Talent Trends 2014: What's on the Minds of the Professional Workforce, 2014; Gallup State of the Global Workplace Report: Employee Engagement Insights for Business Leaders Worldwide," 2013, accessed October 18, 2014, https://business.linkedin.com/content/dam/business/talent-solutions/global/en_US/c/pdfs/linkedin-talent-trends-2014-en-us.pdf.

7. Net Impact, "Talent Report: What Workers Want in 2012," accessed August 14, 2014, https://netimpact.org/sites/default/files/documents/what-workers-want-2012-summary.pdf.

8. Towers Watson, 2012 Global Workforce Study, accessed August 24, 2013, http://www.towerswatson.com/assets/pdf/2012-Towers-Watson-Global-Workforce-Study.pdf.

9. See, for example, Satoris S. Culbertson, Clive J. Fullagar, and Maura J. Mills, "Feeling Good and Doing Great: The Relationship Between Psychological Capital and Well-Being," *Journal of Occupational Health Psychology* 15, no. 4 (October 2010): 421–433.

10. "Our Business," Barry-Wehmiller, accessed May 6, 2015, http://www.barrywehmiller.com/our-business.

11. Author interview with Chapman (CEO and chairman of Barry-Wehmiller), summer 2014.

12. Ibid.

13. "Culture and Values," Alibaba, accessed March 14, 2015, http://www.alibabagroup.com/en/about/culture.

14. Business.asiaone.com; "Inside Alibaba's 'Kung Fu' Culture," by China Daily/Asia News Network, accessed March 14, 2015, http://business.asiaone.com/news/inside-alibabas-kung-fu-culture.

15. Paul Jankowski, "What the Core Values of Alibaba Can Teach Us," Forbes.com, accessed March 14, 2015, http://www.forbes.com/sites/pauljankowski/2014/09/30/what-the-core-values-of-alibaba-can-teach-us/.

16. Ibid.

17. Ibid.

18. Matthew D. Lieberman, *Social: Why Our Brains Are Wired to Connect* (New York: Crown Publishers, 2013), 18–21, 241–246.

19. Barbara L. Fredrickson, "The Role of Positive Emotions in Positive Psychology: The Broaden-and-Build Theory of Positive Emotions," *American Psychologist* 56, no. 3 (March 2001): 218–226.

20. Carroll E. Izard, "Basic Emotions, Natural Kinds, Emotions, Schemas, and a New Paradigm," *Association for Psychological Science* 2, no. 3 (2007): 260–280.

21. Barbara Fredrickson, "What Good Are Positive Emotions?" *Review of General Psychology*, 2, no. 3, 300–319.

22. Personal correspondence with Rich Sheridan via email with the author, October 15, 2014.

23. Yochai Benkler, "The Unselfish Gene," *Harvard Business Review* (July–August 2011), 77–85.

24. "Market Basket Sale to Former Boss Ends Bitter Dispute," by BBC, accessed August 30, 2014, http://www.bbc.com/news/business-28972536. Forbes.com; "Market Basket: The Return of Boom Activism by Next Avenue, accessed August 30, 2014, http://www.forbes.com/sites/nextavenue/2014/08/28/market-basket-the-return-of-boomer-activism/.

25. Denise Lavoie, Associated Press, "Market Basket Drama Ends as Deal Reached to Sell New England Supermarket Chain to Former CEO," *Huffington Post,* August 8, 2014, accessed August 30, 2014, http://www.huffingtonpost.com/2014/08/27/market-basket-drama_n_5726776.html; "Market Basket Sale to Former Boss Ends Bitter Dispute," bbc.com, August 28, 2014, accessed August 30, 2014, http://www.bbc.com/news/business-28972536; Next Avenue, "Market Basket: The Return of Boomer Activism," Forbes.com, August 28, 2014, accessed August 30, 2014, http://www.forbes.com/sites/nextavenue/2014/08/28/market-basket-the-return-of-boomer-activism/; Raw Video: Arthur T. Demoulas On Return To Market Basket, YouTube video, 12:24, posted by WMUR-TV, August 28, 2014, https://www.youtube.com/watch?v=-0vYmy7tIPs.

26. Luck Companies, *Values Based Leadership Journal,* internal resource for company employees shared with the author.

27. Deloitte, "Mind the Gaps: The 2015 Deloitte Millennial Survey-Executive Summary," accessed March 20, 2015, http://www2.deloitte.com/content/dam/Deloitte/global/Documents/About-Deloitte/gx-wef-2015-millennial-survey-executivesummary.pdf.

28. Deloitte, "Culture of Purpose: A Business Imperative 2013 Core Beliefs and Culture Survey," accessed December 12, 2013, https://www2.deloitte.com/content/dam/Deloitte/us/Documents/about-deloitte/us-leadership-2013-core-beliefs-culture-survey-051613.pdf.

29. McKinsey & Company, "Increasing the 'Meaning Quotient' of Work," by Susie Cranston and Scott Keller, accessed June 22, 2014, http://www.mckinsey.com/insights/organization/increasing_the_meaning_quotient_of_work.

30. McKinsey & Company, "McKinsey Global Survey Results: The Value of Centered Leadership," by Joanna Barsh, Josephine Mogelof, and Caroline Webb, accessed November 1, 2014, http://www.mckinsey.com/insights/leading_in_the_21st_century/the_value_of_centered_leadership_mckinsey_global_survey_results. The dimensions in the study of centered leadership by Barsh and her colleagues include meaning, framing, connecting, engaging, and energizing. Barsh also has a book exploring the dimensions in depth: *Centered Leadership* (New York: Crown Publishing, 2014).

31. Ken Blanchard Companies, "Employee Work Passion: What's Important in Creating a Motivating Work Environment and Whose Job Is It?" retrieved July 10, 2011, http://www.kenblanchard.com/img/pub/Blanchard_Employee_Passion_Vol_3.pdf.

32. Timothy Stenovec, "One Reason for Netflix's Success—It Treats Employees Like Grownups," *Huffington Post,* February 27, 2015, updated March 3, 2015, accessed March 2, 2015, http://www.huffingtonpost.com/2015/02/27/netflix-culture-deck-success_n_6763716.html.

33. Netflix Culture Deck version 2, accessed August 9, 2014, http://www.slideshare.net/reed2001/culture-1798664.

34. Ibid.

35. Deloitte Economics Intelligence Unit, "Societal Purpose: A Journey in Its Early Stages," January 2012, accessed March 20, 2015, http://www.economistinsights.com/sites/default/files/downloads/EIU_Societal_Purpose_web.pdf.

36. Personal correspondence with Mark Fernandes via email to the author, January 28, 2015.

37. The model for workplace optimism was inspired by two research topics in the field of positive psychology and positive organizational behavior: psychological capital and eudaimonia well-being. Carol Ryff's work on well-being has profoundly shaped my understanding of workplace optimism and what it looks like. So, too, has Fred Luthan's work on positive organizational behavior and psychological capital. Both have published a multitude of papers on these topics.

CHAPTER 2: DESTRUCTIVE MANAGEMENT

1. Mayo Clinic, "Antisocial Personality Disorder," Mayclinic.org, April 12, 2013, accessed March 21, 2015, http://www.mayoclinic.org/diseases-conditions/antisocial-personality-disorder/basics/definition/con-20027920.

2. Adam Grant, *Give and Take: A Revolutionary Approach to Success* (New York: Viking), 130.

3. Joke author unknown. See Anti.joke.com, accessed May 10, 2015, http://anti-joke.com/anti-joke/page/3632-man-walks-into-a-bar-and-pauses-at-the-other-end-of-the-bar-there-s-this-guy-with-a-big.

4. Douglas McGregor, *The Human Side of Enterprise*, annotated (New York: McGraw-Hill, 2006), 69.

5. Author interview with Cassie Whitlock, August 8, 2014.

6. Edward L. Deci and Richard M. Ryan, "Self-Determination Theory: A Macrotheory of Human Motivation, Development, and Health," *Canadian Psychology*, 49, no. 3 (2008): 182–185.

7. Douglas LaBier, "What Psychological Health Looks Like," *Huffington Post*, January 21, 2011, accessed May 10, 2015, http://www.huffingtonpost.com/douglas-labier/psychological-health_b_811540.html.

8. Deci and Ryan, "Self-Determination Theory," 182–185.

9. Net Impact, "Talent Report: What Workers Want in 2012," accessed August 14, 2014, https://netimpact.org/research-and-publications/talent-report-what-workers-want-in-2012; Price Waterhouse Cooper, "PwC's NextGen: A Global Generational Study" accessed August 14, 2014, http://www.pwc.com/en_GX/gx/hr-management-services/pdf/pwc-nextgen-study-2013.pdf.

10. Roy Baumeister and Mark R. Leary, "The Need to Belong: Desire for Interpersonal Attachments as a Fundamental Human Motivation," *Psychological Bulletin* 117, no. 3 (1995): 497–529.

11. Jane O'Reilly, Sandra L. Robinson, Jennifer L. Berdahl, and Sara Banki, "Is Negative Attention Better Than No Attention?: The Comparative Effects of Ostracism and Harassment at Work," *Organization Science* (April 2014): 1–20.

12. Carol Ryff's work has influenced my understanding of well-being and its role in workplace optimism. Her body of work on the topic of psychological well-being is expansive and illuminating. Here are some of her works that informed this section: "Psychological Well-Being Revisited: Advances in the Science and Practice of Eudaimonia," *Psychotherapy and Psychosomatics* 83, no. 1 (November 19, 2013): 10–28; Carol D. Ryff and Burton H. Singer, "Know Thyself and Become What You Are: A Eudaimonic Approach to Psychological Well-Being," *Journal of Happiness Studies* 9 (2008): 13–39; "Happiness Is Everything, or Is It?: Explorations on the Meaning of Psychological Well-Being," *Journal of Personality and Social Psychology* 57, no. 6 (1989): 1069–1081.

13. The Jensen Group, "The Future of Work: Making the Future Work 2015–2020 and Decades to Come," accessed October 2014, http://www.simpler work.com/futureofwork/.

14. Carol S. Dweck, *Mindset: The New Psychology of Success—Parenting, Business, School, Relationships* (New York: Ballantine, 2006), 3–44.

15. Ibid., 7, 21, 41.

16. Stephen R. Covey, *The 7 Habits of Highly Effective People: Powerful Lessons in Personal Change* (New York: Simon & Schuster, 2013), 249.

17. Researchers Fred Luthans, James Avey, and Jaime Patera explain that breaking goals into smaller ones helps generate hope in your team members. This provides encouragement and believability that the goal is possible. See "Experimental Analysis of a Web-Based Training Intervention to Develop Positive Psychological Capital," *Academy of Management Learning & Education* 7, no. 2 (2008): 209–221.

18. Thomas Teal, "The Human Side of Management," *Harvard Business Review* (November–December 1996): 3–10.

19. Peter Block, *Stewardship: Choosing Service over Self-Interest* (San Francisco: Berrett-Koehler, 1993), xx.

CHAPTER 3: THE POWER OF CONTAGIOUS EMOTIONS

1. Researchers Todd Kashdan and Robert Biswas-Diener argue that we need to embrace some of the darker sides of our emotions, like selfishness. In part, this helps us better meet the demands placed on us in work and in life. Todd Kashdan and Robert Biswas-Diener, *The Upside of Your Dark Side: Why Being Your Whole Self—Not Just Your "Good" Self—Drives Success and Fulfillment* (New York: Hudson Street Press, 2014).

2. The concept of unplanned giving is based on Jennifer George and Arthur Brief's work on organizational spontaneity, specifically their 1992 article "Feeling Good–Doing Good: A Conceptual Analysis of the Mood at Work–Organizational Spontaneity Relationship," *Psychological Bulletin* 112, no. 2 (1992): 310–329.

3. Carol Ryff, "Eudaemonic Well-Being and Health: Mapping Consequences of Self-Realization," in A. S. Waterman, ed., *The Best Within Us: Positive Psychology Perspectives on Eudaimonia* (Washington, DC: American Psychological Association, 2013), 77–79.

4. Alan S. Waterman, "Two Conceptions of Happiness: Contrasts of Personal Expression (Eudaimonia) and Hedonic Enjoyment," *Journal of Personality and Social Psychology* 64, no. 4 (1993): 681

5. Alan S. Waterman, "Personal Expressiveness: Philosophical and Psychological Foundations," *Journal of Mind and Behavior* 11, no. 1 (Winter 1990): 47.

6. Stewart D. Friedman, *Leading the Life You Want: Skills for Integrating Work and Life* (Boston: Harvard Business Review Press, 2014) 8.

7. Waterman, "Personal Expressiveness," 54.

8. Sigal G. Barsade, "The Ripple Effect: Emotional Contagion and Its Influence on Group Behavior," *Administrative Science Quarterly* 47 (2002): 644–675.

9. Barbara Fredrickson, *Positivity: Top-Notch Research Reveals the 3-to-1 Ratio That Will Change Your Life* (New York: Three Rivers Press), 21.

10. Catherine Ryan Hyde, *Pay It Forward* (New York: Simon & Schuster, 2014).

11. Barbara L. Fredrickson, "Why Positive Emotions Matter in Organizations: Lessons from the Broaden-and-Build Model," *The Psychologist-Manager Journal* 4, no. 2 (2000): 134.

12. Fredrickson, *Positivity*, 40–47.

13. MagicValley.com, "Paraplegic Canadian BASE Jumper Returns to Bridge That Nearly Killed Him," by Brian Smith, July 29, 2014, accessed August 29, 2014, http://magicvalley.com/news/local/paraplegic-canadian-base-jumper-returns-to-bridge-that-nearly-killed/article_d0cebfcc-16dc-11e4-b5b8-0019bb2963f4.html.

14. Root Inc., "America's Workforce: A Revealing Account of What Employees Really Think About Today's Workplace," accessed April 29, 2013, http://www.rootinc.com/pdfs/campaign/Americas_Workforce.pdf.

15. Fredrickson, "Why Positive Emotions Matter in Organizations," 139.

CHAPTER 4: THE DOWNSIDE OF OPTIMISM: MISSTEPS AND EXCESS

1. Patrick Lencioni on the Four Disciplines of Healthy Organizations by World of Business Ideas, accessed January 2014, https://www.youtube.com/watch?v=SJAeFnd3QWE.

2. Theresa M. Amabile and Steven J. Kramer, "Inner Work Life: Understanding the Subtext of Business Performance," *Harvard Business Review* (May 2007): 1–12.

3. Hay Group, "The New Rules of Engagement," 2014, accessed August 14, 2014, 12, http://f.datasrvr.com/fr1/414/25154/Hay_Group_New_Rules_of_Engagement_Report.pdf.

4. David Goss, "Reconsidering Schumpeterian Opportunities: The Contribution of Interaction Ritual Chain Theory," *International Journal of Entrepreneurial Research and Behavior* 13, no. 1 (2007): 4.

5. Ibid., 5.

6. Ibid., 4.

7. Ibid., 4.

8. Ibid., 5.

9. Antonella Delle Fave, Ingrid Brdar, Teresa Freire, Dianne Vella-Brodrick, and Marié P. Wissing, "The Eudaimonic and Hedonic Components of Happiness: Qualitative and Quantitative Findings," *Social Indicator Research* 100 (2011): 185–207.

10. Hay Group, Sharon Crabtree and Michael Dodds, "Creating the Climate to Get the Most from Your Team: Helping Leaders Create High-Performing Organizations," November 2011, accessed August 24, 2014, http://www.

thecqi.org/Documents/community/WQD/Sellafield%20presentations%20
2011/Sharon%20Crabtree-Mike%20Dodds.pdf.

11. Hay Group, "Organizational Climate Survey (OCS)," accessed August 24, 2014, http://www.haygroup.com/leadershipandtalentondemand/ourprod ucts/item_details.aspx?itemid=51&type=1&t=2.

12. Gary Hamel, "Reinventing Management at the Mashup: Architect & Ideol-ogy," *MixMashUp* (blog), November 7, 2014, accessed November 22, 2014, http://www.mixmashup.org/blog/reinventing-management-mashup-archi tecture-ideology.

CHAPTER 5: VALUES-BASED LEADERSHIP

1. Net Impact, "Talent Report: What Workers Want in 2012," accessed August 14, 2014, https://netimpact.org/sites/default/files/documents/what-work ers-want-2012-summary.pdf.

2. Arthur P. Brief, Janet M. Dukerich, Paul R. Brown, and Joan F. Brett, "What's Wrong with the Treadway Commision Report?: Experimental Analyses of the Effects of Personal Values and Codes of Conduct on Fraudulent Financial Reporting," *Journal of Business Ethics* 15 (1996): 183–198.

3. From an internal presentation shared with the author by Luck Companies in December 2014.

4. Ibid.

5. Ibid.

6. Ibid.

7. Author conversation with Mark Fernandes, March 30, 2015.

8. Alan S. Waterman, "Personal Expressiveness: Philosophical and Psychologi-cal Foundations," *Journal of Mind and Behavior* 11, no. 1 (Winter 1990): 47.

9. Author interview with Danielle Aaronson, August 22, 2014.

10. Author interview with Bob Chapman (CEO and Chairman of Barry-Weh-miller), summer 2014.

11. Ibid.

12. Ibid.

13. Waterman, "Personal Expressiveness."

14. Alan S. Waterman, "Eudaimonic Identity Theory: Identity as Self-Discovery," in Seth J. Schwartz, Koen Luyckx, and Vivian L. Vignoles, eds., *Handbook of Identity Theory and Research* (New York: Springer-Verlag, 2011), 357–379.

15. Towers Watson, "Balancing Employer and Employee Priorities," July 2014, accessed December 13, 2014, http://www.towerswatson.com/en/Insights/ IC-Types/Survey-Research-Results/2014/07/balancing-employer-and-employee-priorities.

16. Peter Drucker, "Managing Oneself," *Harvard Business Review* (January 2005): 1–12.

CHAPTER 6: IT ALL STARTS WITH PURPOSE

1. Toshimasa Sone et al., "Sense of Life Worth Living (Ikigai) and Mortality in Japan: Ohsaki Study," *American Psychosomatic Society* 70 (2008): 709–715.

2. Stacey M. Schaefer et al., "Purpose in Life Predicts Better Emotional Recovery from Negative Stimuli," *PLos /One,* 8 no. 11 (2013): 1–9.

3. Ibid., 1–9.

4. Todd B. Kashdan and Patrick E. McKnight, "Origins of Purpose in Life: Refining Our Understanding of a Life Well Lived," *Psychological Topics* 18, no. 2 (2009): 303–316.

5. Schaefer et al., "Purpose in Life," 1–9.

6. Ibid., 7–8.

7. Nick Craig and Scott Snook, "From Purpose to Impact," *Harvard Business Review* (May 2014): 106–111.

8. Karen Christensen, "'Thought Leader' interview with Paul Poleman," *Rotman Management* (Winter 2015): 12–17.

9. Todd B. Kashdan and Patrick E. McKnight, "Purpose in Life as a System That Creates and Sustains Health and Well-Being: An Integrative, Testable Theory," *Review of General Psychology* 13, no. 3 (2009): 242–251.

10. Some of the questions were developed based on a framework described in Kashdan and McKnight, "Origins of Purpose in Life."

11. Paul Polman, "Business, Society, and the Future of Capitalism," McKinsey & Company, May 2014, accessed December 28, 2014, http://www.mckinsey.com/Insights/Sustainability/Business_society_and_the_future_of_capitalism?cid=other-eml-alt-mkq-mck-oth-1405.

12. Phillip Haid, "Unilever's Corporate Challenge: Find Purpose or Perish," *Financial Post*, May 28, 2014, accessed December 28, 2014, http://business.financialpost.com/2014/05/28/unilevers-corporate-challenge-find-purpose-or-perish/.

13. Polman, "Business, Society, and the Future of Capitalism."

14. Author interview with Alice Cabrera, September 4, 2014.

15. Malcolm G. Patterson, et al. "Validating the Organizational Climate Measure: Links to Managerial Practices, Productivity and Innovation," *Journal of Organizational Behavior* 26 (2005): 379–408.

16. Lynda Gratton, "Building Resilience in a Fragile World," *Rotman Management* (Winter 2015): 47–51.

17. Details about Re-Mission are from HopeLab's website; see http://www.hopelab.org/innovative-solutions/re-mission-2/.

18. Author interview with Pat Christen, September 4, 2014. More information about HopeLab's work in resilience is at http://www.hopelab.org/innovative-solutions/resilience-initiative/.

19. Author interview with Pat Christen, September 4, 2014.

20. Each week a small team of HopeLab employees is responsible for making healthy snacks for colleagues. For the making of a flash mob surprise dance for a colleague's last day at HopeLab, see https://www.youtube.com/watch?v=j0Y-XyjycPo.

21. Nick Craig and Scott Snook, "From Purpose to Impact," *Harvard Business Review* (May 2014): 106–111.

22. Deloitte, "Culture of Purpose: A Business Imperative 2013 Core Beliefs and Culture Survey," accessed December 12, 2013, https://www2.deloitte.com/content/dam/Deloitte/us/Documents/about-deloitte/us-leadership-2013-core-beliefs-culture-survey-051613.pdf.

23. Robert Safian, "Generation Flux's Secret Weapon," *Fast Company*, November

2014, accessed December 3, 2014, http://www.fastcompany.com/3035975/generation-flux/find-your-mission.

24. The Jensen Group, "The Future of Work: Making the Future Work 2015–2020 and Decades to Come," accessed October 2014, http://www.simplerwork.com/futureofwork/.

25. Net Impact, "Talent Report: What Workers Want in 2012," accessed August 14, 2014, https://netimpact.org/sites/default/files/documents/what-workers-want-2012-summary.pdf.

26. Ibid.

CHAPTER 7: THE MEANING MAKERS

1. Antonella Delle Fave, Ingrid Brdar, Teresa Freire, Dianne Vella-Brodrick, and Marié P. Wissing, "The Eudaimonic and Hedonic Components of Happiness: Qualitative and Quantitative Findings," *Social Indicators Research* 100 (2011): 185–207.

2. Joanna Barsh, Josephine Mogelof, and Caroline Webb, "McKinsey Global Survey Results: The Value of Centered Leadership," McKinsey & Company, October 2010, accessed November 1, 2014, http://www.mckinsey.com/insights/leading_in_the_21st_century/the_value_of_centered_leadership_mckinsey_global_survey_results.

3. Alexandra Levit and Dr. Sanja Licina, "How the Recession Shaped Millennial and Hiring Manager Attitudes About Millennials' Future Careers," Career Advisory Board, presented by DeVry University, 2011, accessed October 26, 2014, http://www.careeradvisoryboard.org/public/uploads/2011/10/ Future-of- Millennial-Careers-Report.pdf.

4. Emily Esfahani Smith and Jennifer L. Aaker, "Millennial Searchers," New YorkTimes.com, November 30, 2014, accessed October 6, 2014, http://www.nytimes.com/2013/12/01/opinion/sunday/millennial-searchers.html?smid=tw-share&_r=1.

5. Roy Baumeister, Kathleen D. Vohs, Jennifer L. Aaker, and Emily N. Garbinsky, "Some Key Differences Between a Happy Life and a Meaningful Life," *Journal of Positive Psychology* 8, no. 6 (2013): 505–516.

6. Delle Fave et al., "The Eudaimonic and Hedonic Components of Happiness."

7. Author interview with Ryan Sanders at BambooHR, August 8, 2014.

8. Jim Asplund, "When Americans Use Their Strengths More, They Stress Less," Gallup, September 27, 2012, accessed December 10, 2014, http://www.gallup.com/poll/157679/americans-strengths-stress-less.aspx.

9. Author interview with Bob Chapman (Barry Wehmiller CEO and chairman), summer 2014.

10. Ken Blanchard Companies, "Creating a Motivating Work Environment," 2009, accessed December 2, 2012, http://www.kenblanchard.com/img/pub/Blanchard_Creating_a_Motivating_Work_Environment.pdf.

11. Barbara L. Fredrickson, "Why Positive Emotions Matter in Organizations: Lessons from the Broaden-and-Build Model," *The Psychologist-Manager Journal* 4, no. 2 (2000): 131–142.

12. Fredrickson's *Positivity* is essential reading for leaders who want to understand how creating positive emotions in people can help optimism in the workplace emerge. She lists 10 forms of positivity: joy, gratitude, serenity, interest, hope, pride, amusement, inspiration, awe, and love. 40–47.

13. Kare Anderson, *Getting What You Want: How to Reach Agreement and Resolve Conflict Every Time* (New York: Plume, 1994).

14. Author interview with Alice Cabrera of HopeLab, September 4, 2014.

15. S. Karpman, "Fairy Tales and Script Drama Analysis," *Transactional Analysis Bulletin* 7, no. 26 (1968): 39–43.

16. James Kouzes and Barry Posner, *The Leadership Challenge: How to Make Extraordinary Things Happen in Organizations*, 5th ed. (San Francisco: Jossey-Bass, 2012), 40.

17. Max DePree, *Leadership Is an Art* (New York: Currency Book, 2004), Kindle edition.

18. Chip Conley, *Peak: How Great Companies Get Their Mojo from Maslow* (San Francisco: Jossey-Bass, 2007), 83.

19. Neel Burton, M.D., "Our Hierarchy of Needs: Why True Freedom Is a Luxury of the Mind," PsychologyToday.com, accessed May 16, 2015, https://www.psychologytoday.com/blog/hide-and-seek/201205/our-hierarchy-needs.

20. Richard M. Ryan and Edward L. Deci, "Intrinsic and Extrinsic Motivations: Classic Definitions and New Directions," *Contemporary Educational Psychology* 25 (2000): 54–67.

21. Paul Taylor and Scott Keeter, eds. "Confident. Connected. Open to Change," Pew Research Center, February 2010, accessed January 1, 2015, http://www.pewresearch.org/daily-number/the-millennial-count/.

22. Sally Helgesen, "How to Create Meaning at Work When the Outcome Isn't Always Meaningful," *strategy+business* (blog), January 14, 2014, accessed January 20, 2014, http://www.strategy-business.com/blog/How-to-Create-Meaning-at-Work-When-the-Outcome-Isnt-Always-Meaningful.

23. Roy Baumeister, Kathleen D. Vohs, Jennifer L. Aaker, and Emily N. Garbinsky, "Some Key Differences Between a Happy Life and a Meaningful Life," *Journal of Positive Psychology* 8, no. 6 (2013): 5.

24. Ibid., 4.

CHAPTER 8: WE MUST CHANGE THE WAY WE WORK

1. Adam M. Grant, "Relational Job Design and the Motivation to Make a Prosocial Difference," *Academy of Management Review* 32, no. 2 (2007): 393.

2. *Performance with Purpose Sustainability Report*, PepsiCo report, 2013, 48, accessed May 3, 2015, http://www.pepsico.com/docs/album/sustainability-reporting/pep_2013_sustainability_report.pdf.

3. Justin M. Berg, Amy Wrzesniewski, and Jane E. Dutton, "Perceiving and Responding to Challenges in Job Crafting at Different Ranks: When Proactivity Requires Adaptivity," *Journal of Organizational Behavior*, 31 (2010): 158–186.

4. David Gelles, "At Aetna, a C.E.O.'s Management by Mantra," *New York Times*, February 25, 2015, accessed April 5, 2015, http://www.nytimes.com/2015/03/01/business/at-aetna-a-ceos-management-by-mantra.html?_r=0.

5. John Hagel, John Seely Brown, and Tamara Samoylova, "Unlocking the Passion of the Explorer," Deloitte Center for the Edge, 2013, accessed June 3,

2014, http://d2mtr37y39tpbu.cloudfront.net/wp-content/uploads/2013/09/
DUP 402_Worker-Passion_vFINAL3.pdf.

6. Ibid.

7. In a keynote address on June 12, 2013, given to employees at technology company, SAP, author Seth Godin distinguished two human traits that uphold the connection revolution: generosity and art. Accessed January 16, 2015, https://www.youtube.com/watch?v=sKXZgTzEyWY.

8. The Jensen Group, "The Future of Work: Making the Future Work 2015–2020 and Decades to Come," accessed October 2014, http://www.simpler work.com/futureofwork/.

9. Ibid.

10. Dana Unger, Cornelia Niessen, Sabine Sonnentag, and Angela Neff, "A Question of Time: Daily Time Allocation Between Work and Private Life," *Journal of Occupational and Organizational Psychology* 87 (2014): 158–176.

11. Ibid.

12. Ibid., 164–165.

13. Great Place to Work Institute, "5 Lessons for Leaders as They Build a Great Workplace," 2014, accessed January 17, 2015, http://createyours.greatpla cetowork.com/rs/greatplacetowork/images/2014-5-Lessons-for-Leaders-whitepaper-fnl.pdf?utm_source=marketo&utm_medium=email&utm_ content=whitepaper-pdf-download&utm_campaign=5-lessons-for-leaders&mkt_tok=3RkMMJWWfF9wsRojvqTJZKXonjHpfsX96uQoXK+3l MI/0ER3fOvrPUfGjI4ESMJgI+SLDwEYGJlv6SgFQrnAMbduzrgMXhM=.

14. Ibid., 7.

15. Ibid., 14.

16. Great Place to Work Institute, "The Dawn of the Great Workplace Era," 2014, accessed December 29, 2014, http://www.greatplacetowork.net/storage/ documents/Publications_Documents/The_Dawn_of_the_Great_Work place_Era.pdf.

17. Albert Bandura, "Social Cognitive Theory: An Agentic Perspective," *Annual Review of Psychology* 52 (2001): 1–26.

18. Reid Hoffman, Ben Casnocha, and Chris Yeh, *The Alliance: Managing Talent in the Networked Age* (Boston: Harvard Business Review Press), 7–9, 22–55.

19. Great Place to Work Institute, "5 Lessons for Leaders as They Build a Great Workplace," 7.

20. Jessica Rohman, "Lessons for Leaders as They Build a Great Workplace," *Great Place to Work* (blog), August 20, 2014, accessed January 17, 2014, http://www.greatplacetowork.com/publications-and-events/blogs-and-news/2731-build-a-great-workplace-whitepaper.

21. Teresa Amabile and Steven Kramer, *The Progress Principle: Using Small Wins to Ignite Joy, Engagement, and Creativity at Work* (Boston: Harvard Business Review Press, 2011), Kindle edition.

22. Author interview with Bob Chapman (CEO and Chairman of Barry-Wehmiller), summer 2014.

23. Net Impact, "Talent Report: What Workers Want in 2012," accessed August 14, 2014, https://netimpact.org/sites/default/files/documents/what-work ers-want-2012-summary.pdf.

24. Bob Chapman, "Truly Human Leadership." June 20, 2012, TEDXScottAFB

video, 22:02, posted by TEDx Talks, https://www.youtube.com/watch?v=njn-lIEv1LU.

CHAPTER 9: HUMAN-CENTERED LEADERSHIP

1. Author interview with Charlie Luck, August 21, 2014.
2. Emily D. Heaphy and Jane E. Dutton, "Positive Social Interactions and the Human Body at Work: Living Organizations and Physiology," *Academy of Management Review* 33, no. 1 (2008): 150.
3. Author interview with Charlie Luck, August 21, 2014.
4. Ed Frauenheim, "A Killer Culture Keeps Google Vital," *Great Rated* (blog), December 1, 2014, accessed January 17, 2015, http://us.greatrated.com/blog/a-killer-culture-keeps-google-vital.
5. Towers Watson, "2012 Global Workforce Study: Engagement at Risk: Driving Strong Performance in a Volatile Global Environment," accessed August 24, 2013, http://www.towerswatson.com/assets/pdf/2012-Towers-Watson-Glo bal-Workforce-Study.pdf.
6. Root Inc., "America's Workforce: A Revealing Account of What Employees Really Think About Today's Workplace," (2013) accessed April 29, 2013, http://www.rootinc.com/pdfs/campaign/Americas_Workforce.pdf.
7. Towers Watson, "A Global Workforce Study: At a Glance," 2014, accessed December 13, 2014, http://www.towerswatson.com/en-US/Insights/IC-Types/Survey-Research-Results/2014/08/the-2014-global-workforce-study.
8. Root Inc., "America's Workforce: A Revealing Account of What Employees Really Think About Today's Workplace."
9. David Gelles, "At Aetna, A C.E.O.'s Management by Mantra," NYTimes.com, February 27, 2015, accessed April 5, 2015, http://www.nytimes.com/2015/03/01/business/at-aetna-a-ceos-management-by-mantra.html?_r=0.
10. Brian Mahoney, "Aetna Sets Wage Floor," Politico, January 13, 2015, accessed April 5, 2015, http://www.politico.com/morningshift/0115/morningshift 16704 .html.
11. *Guiding Principles of Leadership* is an internal Barry-Wehmiller document shared with the author in 2014.
12. Author interview with Rosa Lopez of HopeLab, September 15, 2014.
13. Denise Fairhurst and Justine O'Connor, "Employee Well-Being: Taking Engagement and Performance to the Next Level," Towers Watson, 2010, accessed March 6, 2012, http://www.towerswatson.com/en/Insights/News letters/Global/strategy-at-work/2010/Employee-Well-Being-Taking-Engagement-and-Performance-to-the-Next-Level.
14. Antonella Delle Fave, Ingrid Brdar, Teresa Freire, Dianne Vella-Brodrick, and Marié P. Wissing, "The Eudaimonic and Hedonic Components of Happiness: Qualitative and Quantitative Findings," *Social Indicators Research*, 100 (2011): 185–207.
15. Author interview with Dawn Hack of Luck Companies, August 21, 2014.
16. Justin M. Berg, Amy Wrzesniewski, and Jane E. Dutton, "Perceiving and Responding to Challenges in Job Crafting at Different Ranks: When Proac-

tivity Requires Adaptivity," *Journal of Organizational Behavior* 31 (2010): 158–186.

17. Aaron Hurst, *The Purpose Economy*, Pre-publication Beta Edition (Idaho: Elevate Media, 2013), 33.

18. Paul Jaminet's early research on relationship economics is fascinating to read. While there is little of it, Jaminet did good work examining the economics of relationships and their importance to business. His research is somewhat academic, but there are nuggets of wisdom worth finding in this social media age we live in. You can read his work at http://www.relationshipeconomics.com/introduction.htm.

19. Author interview with Bob Chapman (CEO and Chairman of Barry-Wehmiller), summer 2014.

20. Robert I. Sutton, "Why Good Bosses Tune in to Their People," *McKinsey Quarterly* (August 2010): 8.

21. Barbara L. Fredrickson, "Why Positive Emotions Matter in Organizations: Lessons from the Broaden-and-Build Model," *The Psychologist-Manager Journal* 4, no. 2 (2000): 131.

22. Sigal G. Barsade, "The Ripple Effect: Emotional Contagion and Its Influence on Group Behavior," *Administrative Science Quarterly* 47 (2002): 644–675.

23. Author interview with Jeremy Bowers of BambooHR, August 7, 2014.

24. Weber Shandwick and KRC Research, "Employee Rising: Seizing the Opportunity in Employee Activism," 2014, accessed 2014, http://webershandwick.asia/wp-content/uploads/2014/04/WS-EmployeeActivism-report_A4-APAC1.pdf.

25. Bob Chapman, "The Power of Thanks," *Truly Human Leadership* (blog), November 16, 2012, accessed January 25, 2015, http://www.trulyhumanleader ship.com/?p=313.

CHAPTER 10: NEXT COMES TRUST: CREATING COMMUNITY

1. Matthew D. Lieberman, *Social: Why Our Brains Are Wired to Connect* (New York: Crown Publishers, 2013), 81.

2. Alex "Sandy" Pentland, "The New Science of Building Great Teams," *Harvard Business Review* (April 2012): 1–11.

3. Ben Warber, Jennifer Magnolfi, and Greg Lindsay, "Workspaces That Move People," *Harvard Business Review* (October 2014): 69–77.

4. Jane E. Dutton and Emily D. Heaphy, "The Power of High-Quality Connections," in K. Cameron, J. Dutton, and R. Quinn, eds., *Positive Organizational Scholarship* (San Francisco: Berrett-Koehler, 2003), 275.

5. Paul Zak, "The Neurobiology of Trust," *Scientific American* (June 2008): 88–95; Paul Zak, "Trust, Morality and Oxytocin," filmed July 2011, TED video, 16:34, https://www.ted.com/talks/paul_zak_trust_morality_and_oxytocin; Michael Kosfeld, "Oxytocin Increases Trust in Humans," *Nature* 435, no. 2 (2005): 673–677; Paul Zak, "Oxytocin Is Associated with Human Trustworthiness," *Hormones and Behavior* 48 (2005): 522–527; Paul J. Zak, Angela A. Stanton, and Sheila Ahmadi, "Oxytocin Increases Generosity in Humans," *PLoS One* 2, no. 11 (2007), accessed January 11, 2015, http://jour

nals.plos.org/plosone/article?id=10.1371/journal.pone.0001128#pone-0001128-g001.

6. Jane O'Reilly, Sandra L. Robinson, Jennifer L. Berhahl, and Sara Banki, "Is Negative Attention Better Than No Attention?" *Articles in Advance* (2014): 1–20.

7. Ibid.

8. Roy Baumeister and Mark R. Leary, "The Need to Belong: Desire for Interpersonal Attachments as a Fundamental Human Motivation," *Psychological Bulletin* 117, no. 3 (1995): 497–529.

9. Dutton and Heaphy, "The Power of High-Quality Connections," 268.

10. Nitin Nhoria, Boris Groysberg, and Linda-Eling Lee, "Employee Motivation: A Powerful New Model," *Harvard Business Review* (July–August 2008): 2–3.

11. Zak, "The Neurobiology of Trust," 91.

12. Kare Anderson. *Mutuality Matters: How You Can Create More Opportunity, Adventure & Friendship with Others* (Substantium, 2014), Kindle edition.

CHAPTER 11: THE CULTIVATION OF OPTIMISM

1. Author interview with Ryan Sanders, BambooHR, August 8, 2014.

2. Randall Beck and Jim Harter, "Why Great Managers Are So Rare," March 25, 2014, accessed January 15, 2015, http://www.gallup.com/businessjournal/167975/why-great-managers-rare.aspx.

3. Tom Rath and Barry Conchie, *Strengths Based Leadership* (New York: Gallup Press, 2008), Loc1421–1422, Kindle edition.

4. There are many great resources to learn what your strengths are. In the interest of full disclosure I am accredited to administer Strengthscope assessment. It's an assessment to help you identify your strengths.

5. Amy Y. Ou, Anne S. Tsui, Angelo J. Kinicki, David A. Waldman, Zhixing Xioa, and Lynda Jiwen Song, "Humble Chief Executive Officers' Connections to Top Management Team Integration and Middle Managers' Responses," *Administrative Science Quarterly* 59, no. 1 (2014): 34–72.

6. Ibid.

7. Pope Benedict XVI, "Silence and Word: Path of Evangelization," May 20, 2012, accessed March 3, 2014, http://w2.vatican.va/content/benedict-xvi/en/messages/communications/documents/hf_ben-xvi_mes_20120124_46th-world-communications-day.html

8. Angela L. Duckworth, Christopher Peterson, Michael D. Matthews, and Dennis R. Kelly, "Grit: Perseverance and Passion for Long-Term Goals," *Journal of Personality and Social Psychology* 92, no. 6 (2007): 1087–1101.

9. Katherine R. Von Culin, Eli Tsukayama, and Angela L. Duckworth, "Unpacking Grit: Motivational Correlates of Perseverance and Passion for Long-Term Goals," *Journal of Positive Psychology* (2014): 1–7.

10. Barbara L. Fredrickson, "Why Positive Emotions Matter in Organizations: Lessons from the Broaden-and-Build Model," *The Psychologist-Manager Journal*, 133.

11. Michael A. Cohn, Barbara L. Fredrickson, Stephanie L. Brown, Joseph A. Mikels, and Anne M. Conway, "Happiness Unpacked: Positive Emotions

Increase Life Satisfaction by Building Resilience," *Emotion,* 9 no. 3 (2009): 361–368..

12. My interpretation of sense making was influenced by the work of several researchers. First, Gary Klein, Brian Moon, and Robert R. Hoffman's article "Making Sense of Sensemaking 1: Alternative Perspectives," *The Computer Society* 21, no. 4 (July/August 2006): 70–73, holds insights into the myths of sense making that were helpful in distinguishing my thoughts on the value the skill has to cultivating optimism. Second, work from Karl E. Wick, Kathleen M. Sutcliffe, and David Obsfeld provided a framework to help me understand the actual skills needed for sense making. Their article "Organizing and the Process of Sensemaking," *Organization Science*, 16 no. 4 (July–August 2005): 409–421, is a good read, albeit academic.

13. Author interview with Ryan Sanders of BambooHR. August 8, 2014.

14. Author interview with Ben Peterson of BambooHR, August 8, 2014.

15. Author interview with Dan Cawley of HopeLab, September 5, 2014.

16. Author interview with Rich Sheridan of Menlo Innovations, summer 2014.

17. Author interview with Cassie Whitlock, August 8, 2014.

18. 15Five custom report on the role of workplace optimism based on internal question posed to employees, 2015.

AFTERWORD

1. Jim Collins, keynote address at Global Leadership Summit, August 9, 2012.

2. Lee Scott is a leadership coach and educator. He developed for Sacramento State University a course called Leadership Innovation.

Index